Balanced Mama

by Elizabeth Singler

Paperback ISBN: 978-1-7357140-0-4

eBook ISBN: 978-1-7357140-1-1

Table of Contents

Introduction

"She opens her mouth with wisdom, and the teaching of kindness is on her tongue. She looks well to the ways of her household and does not eat the bread of idleness" (Proverbs 31:26-27, ESV).

Hi there!

It's nice to meet you! I'm Elizabeth. At thirty-five years old, and a bundle of children later, I have discovered that I tend to overdo everything. I understand firsthand about juggling a thousand things at a time, and I'm here to help you get out of the crazy train you might be riding.

The first thing you should know about me is that marriage and motherhood are the most important jobs in my life. Jesus Christ, my husband, and my children are the most important people in my life. Homeschooling is very important to me; I want to train my children with moral values and give them a deeper education than what a public school system allows. I enjoy being in my garden, being creative, going for walks, and spending time outside.

Being a wife and mother has been the most challenging and the most rewarding adventure in my life. I wouldn't want to do anything else. I could live without my garden, time outdoors, any of my businesses, or practically anything else, but I don't know how I'd live without my husband and my children. Since they are my priority, I make everything else in my life revolve around them. Being able to homeschool my children is a blessing for them and also for myself. There is nothing as satisfying as helping your children to grow into intelligent, confident, and successful people who love the Lord.

"I could have no greater joy than to hear that my children are following the truth" (3 John 1:4, NLT).

This book aims to bring you into my life a little bit and give you some wisdom that I've learned along the way. I know many women struggle with finding a balance between caring for themselves, caring for their families, caring for their husbands, teaching their children, trying to pay for things to make ends meet, and making money (either at home or a job). All of these responsibilities can be very stressful for a woman. I want to give you hope, mama. This is for the mama who wants to start a business, homeschool her kids, or take a risk. I want to show you how you can truly do it all and flourish in your relationships. I want to show you how you can be a successful woman, regardless of what life brings you.

As you read these pages, consider that parenting, homeschool, and business are all a fraction of your life. To do all of these well, you need to learn how to balance them throughout your day. This book is meant to be a starting point to show you ways that you can achieve balance in the crazy juggling act of these areas of your journey.

Our world is changing, and many parents are choosing to homeschool their children. Amid homeschoolers, we also have parents starting new careers or beginning businesses to make ends meet. I am thankful that I have had experience in this area to share with you. My greatest desire is for this book to be a resource for success.

Whether you are homeschooling, beginning a business, or both, I know that there is information in this book that can radically change the way that you think and process.

In these pages, I hope you will find rest and peace. I want you to reach your full potential.

Most of my opinions in this book are formed and supported by biblical principles. There is great wisdom the Bible can provide for our lives. However, even if you aren't a Christian, consider that the Bible is an ancient document with timeless wisdom and life suggestions.

In the Bible, 1 Corinthians 4 talks about imitating Paul in his scriptural teaching. While I don't claim to be quite as wise as Paul, I want to give you examples of my own life and personal experiences as a way to teach you how to have balance in your life.

"For the kingdom of God is not just a lot of talk; it is living by God's power" (1 Corinthians 4:20, NLT).

By using biblical principles and applying them to your life, you can live by God's power to have balance. Be the most creative and successful mother, homeschooler, wife, and business owner that you can be. Let's go ahead and get started.

Points to Ponder:

Who are you?

Does a job or position in life define you?

What do you hope to discover by reading this book?

Chapter One

Parenting

I'm going to assume that you are a parent, or you would like to be a parent, if you are reading this book. If these things don't apply to you, I urge you to read on anyway. I'd love to share some fantastic life lessons with anyone willing to listen.

Being a mother can be the most daunting experience of your life. Somehow, we were given a tiny little human to raise and keep alive. On top of keeping the children healthy, we need to nurture them and teach them to become amazing men and women. Loving your child is an incredible task, and it isn't for the faint of heart. It's hard.

However hard it is to be a mother, we need to remember that children are a gift.

Psalm 127:3 says, "Children are a gift from the Lord; they are a reward from him" (NLT).

In this chapter, I want to help you grasp the fantastic gift you've been given, and the effect you have on your children's lives. You are their biggest fan and the most excellent teacher that they could ever have. Whether you homeschool or send to public school, you still teach your children more than anyone else on the planet.

I'm excited to share my thoughts with you, but please remember that I am not a doctor, and I don't have a psychology degree. I'm just an experienced, loving parent giving you practical parenting tips. These parenting tips have changed the way that I view parenting as a whole. My life and parenting style have morphed into something that is truly a blessing, so I'd like to share the essential things that I have found (or have been taught) along the way. This chapter will not give you every answer, but I hope that you will learn something new. Trust in the Lord to guide you to parent your children how they need to be loved.

True Love

In Luke 10, we meet a pair of sisters: Mary and Martha. Martha is an incredible hostess and wants all of her dinner preparations to be perfect for Jesus. However, her sister, Mary, decided to not be bothered by "busy work," and listened to Jesus' teachings. Martha was upset because Mary left her to do all preparations alone. Martha asked Jesus for Mary's help, but instead, He told her that Mary had found the important thing – she realized the precious time with Jesus was to be savored.

When I read this story, I am reminded that we can get caught up in the chaos of life very easily. Like Martha, our homeschool, business, or schedules can get our lives muddied up and too full. We end up missing out on the precious gifts that God has given us when we make ourselves too busy.

To be a balanced mama who still gets work done (like Martha), we must be willing to be still and enjoy life (like Mary). It takes disciplined effort to set our "preparations" aside to enjoy time with our husbands, children, and friends.

When my first baby was born, I was in love. I had dreamed of finally meeting her. I was utterly fascinated with everything baby-related. I spent hours reading books and listening to advice. I had my birth planned out so that I could have the best bonding experience with my child. When she finally came, it was a dream. My delivery was rough, but she was worth it all. I was determined to be the best mom I could be. As my baby became older, I didn't want to miss a single moment, but I got preoccupied with life. On the outside, I was an excellent mom. On the inside, though, I didn't appreciate each moment.

I started my first business, and I felt like I ultimately "found" myself. I finally understood who I was. Having a baby at nineteen was a difficult thing because I was still a baby myself. I, Elizabeth, who had dreamed of being a mother my entire life, was finally living the dream, except I was focused on something else (my business).

I didn't realize that thoughts are a choice. I didn't know that I was choosing to be preoccupied. When I would play with my baby, I was thinking of how to run my business. When we were going for a walk, I was dreaming up new ideas.

Then one day, I realized what I was doing. I was missing it.

When you are raising your children, things come up in your life. You begin new hobbies. You start new projects. Some things are short lived, and others become a complete lifestyle. Sometimes, we get the "Martha syndrome" of too much "stuff" going on. The way to love your children during an adventure is to stop being distracted.

Have you ever talked to someone while they were texting someone else? You know that they aren't truly listening to what you are saying. The same rings true for our children and family. When we are preoccupied with something else, they can sense it, even if you aren't on your phone. They can sense when you are preoccupied with anger. Children sense when you are preoccupied with your job. They even sense when you are preoccupied with motivation to get tasks completed.

Regardless of what is taking your thoughts, I implore you: set it down. When you are with your children, actually be with them. If you need to work, do it at a set time. After work, come "home" and be mom. Take on a "Mary" mentality and enjoy the precious time with your family.

Walking away from a project (even in your thoughts) can be hard sometimes, especially if you are beginning a business, or are obsessing about finding the right homeschool curriculum. However, when you recognize that you are becoming consumed in your thoughts, it's imperative that you jot down your ideas on a notebook and walk away. Stop thinking about your distraction.

Even as I write this book, I have to be mindful to set my thoughts aside to be a mom to my children. However, my world can't revolve around my kids at every moment. Even though Martha was too busy while Jesus was with her, I believe she was valid in her desire to get tasks accomplished. Food will not cook itself, businesses will not run themselves, and school will not be successful without a teacher. There must be a balance between Martha and Mary's preferences.

I tend to be an "all or nothing" kind of girl. My husband calls me a chainsaw...because once I begin, I will blitz through my project, and nothing can stop me. It's a blessing, but also something that I must control.

A chainsaw mindset makes breakthroughs at work quickly and accurately, but sacrifices attention elsewhere. On the other hand, there are also "steak knife" people. The steak knife type of person wants to cut the tree down using a steak knife. This person will only choose to do their project when the children have a babysitter once a month, or when the husband takes them to grandma's for the day. This person isn't practicing a healthy balance either and will not get on their way to success in anything. This mentality shows children that they are the center of your world and that life doesn't exist beyond them. Let me tell you, sister: this isn't the way to live.

To have a healthy balance, you have to have the mindset of an ax. An ax will cut the tree down, but it is a slower and consistent pace. You have time to stop and get the angle right for your blade, and you can land the tree exactly where you want it. It's hard work, but fully capable and consistent with results.

When you choose to have set times to do a project or task and fully devote your mind to the moment with your children, you will be the most consistent. You will genuinely love your children, and you will eventually get your task accomplished. It takes time, but with consistency, your children will be loved, and you will get your tasks complete.

So why do I say that setting our work down is true love? Because Jesus says no one has greater love than he who lays down his life for his friend (John 15:13). When we are willing to lay down our lives for someone else, it is the greatest love you can give. Regardless of the task, business, homeschooling, research, or whatever "it" is, you are loving your family and children when you lay it down. It's important. Do it.

Boundaries

Another way that you can love your children is by recognizing their needs. They have apparent needs like food, water, shelter, and love. But did you realize that they have needs that benefit you? Children have an inner need to love you. They want to be loved, but they also need to love. What is the most excellent way that your children can show you love?

They show love by staying within boundaries.

Children have an inner need to love you.

No matter what age you are, you have boundaries. You have a conscience with a set of God-given boundaries, but you also have human-made boundaries. If you go outside of the boundaries, there is always a consequence.

An example of a God-given boundary is kindness. If you are unkind, your conscience will tell you. It's how God wired us. If you ignore your conscience, you will become numb, and you become even more unkind. Because of unkindness, the consequence will be strained relationships and unhealthy emotions.

An example of a human-made boundary is a speed limit. If you drive five miles over the speed limit, you realize that you might get a ticket. The more that you drive five miles over the speed limit without getting caught, you become numb to getting caught and begin to speed faster. Eventually, you'll be in a heap of trouble when you get busted speeding.

People will push boundaries no matter what. It doesn't matter where you live or the type of people you hang out with. People are people. We are sinners who need a savior.

In the book of Genesis, God gave Adam and Eve boundaries, yet they pushed the boundaries and sinned. God gave them the boundary for their good. By giving Adam and Eve the boundary of not touching the Tree of Life, He gave them a choice to obey. The point was that God made a rule to be followed because He knew what was best for them. When we obey God, we are showing Him that we love and trust Him. Humans need to love.

When you give your children boundaries, they show you love and trust by obeying you. It's how God is with us, and it's how we should be with our children.

What happens when children push your boundaries? There needs to be a hard line. A "no crossing zone" is required. I will not tell you how you should handle consequences in your home, but I will say this: if you want your child to be loving, make them stay in the boundaries. Jesus said if we love Him, we will obey His commandments (John 14:15).

Jesus is our most exceptional example of how to love. Let's run our homes in the same way.

Training

My dog, Miah, is a beautiful Australian Shepherd. She is adorable but high strung. If left to herself, she will jump all over us when we walk in the door. She barks at people walking by and can be pretty rude to visitors. When we go for walks, she can pull us twelve miles per hour if we don't stand our ground.

However, just because she can do these things doesn't mean it's good for her to do them. If we left her to herself, she would be a miserable, painful dog to own. Because of her breeding, she tends to be dominant. That means that even with consistent and constant training, she is always pushing boundaries to see if she can be the boss. It can be aggravating to have to remind her of the rules continually. I love her, but if I would have chosen a different breed, I might have better luck with my training.

Our children are the same as Miah. They will tend toward unpleasant behavior if left to their own. Even with consistent training, they will still push boundaries. However, all children are this way. You can't trade them in for a new breed!

> Proverbs 29:15 says, "...but a child left to himself brings shame to his mother" (ESV).

You can be sure that a dog left to himself (or herself) will be a lousy pet. You can also be sure that a child left to himself (or herself) will bring you trouble in days ahead.

When I discuss Miah's behavior with other dog owners, I get the same responses each time. They all have different methods of consequences, but the training is the same—practice, practice, practice. Start small and work your way up. I can't expect Miah to stay lying down for thirty minutes with guests around before teaching her how to sit for one minute. It's graduated from practicing. That's what training is.

When we train our children, it's the same concept.

Let me give you a child training example.

You bring your trained three-year-old to church. When she passes others, she looks stunning and smiles politely. She has pretty bows in the right place and shiny clean shoes. She smooths her dress when she sits down. She's careful to keep her legs in front of her while sitting. She sings the songs and sits through the service without a peep. After church, she tells you what she learned during service.

This three-year-old has had a lot of training. What do you think allowed her to be such a sweet little thing? Was it natural to her? Not likely. To train your children, you need to practice with them. Create situations where they can practice. By teaching this little person, it allows him/her to accomplish politeness that typical three-year-olds do not possess.

In the above example, I want to point out ways that this girl could have been trained:

> **You brought her to church.** This is probably a regular event. Children excel with having consistent schedules and knowing what you expect. Keeping a consistent schedule is also a form of training.

She smiles politely at others. This is a big one. She practices being kind. She practices smiling at people at the grocery store. She practices smiling at the mailman when he brings packages. She practices smiling at people when they walk by on the street.

She has pretty bows and shiny shoes. She has practiced keeping her hair neat and tidy. She has practiced keeping her church shoes kept apart from her regular play shoes.

She smooths her dress when sitting down. She has learned and practiced this behavior from the way you taught her, and watching you do it. You practice this routine at dinner every day.

She is careful to keep her legs in front while sitting. During family time and mealtimes, you practice how to sit ladylike.

She sings the songs. Is she confident with the songs? Maybe because you play them at home and she practices them. She is confident to sing because you practice with her all the time, and she sees you singing.

She sits through the service without a peep. She has had plenty of practice at sitting time. She has practiced from five minutes up to sixty minutes of sitting still and is prepared for anything.

She tells you about what she learned. She practices telling you things all day long. You practice by asking her what she learns in school. You practice by discussing hard topics at home. You practice by asking her pointed questions when she doesn't seem to be paying attention.

Do you see how simple things can become ingrained into your children to make them a better person? Do you see how simple training can affect their lives for the better?

Proverbs 22:6 says, "Train up a child in the way he should go; even when he is old, he will not depart from it" (NKJV).

Just as it is easiest to start training a puppy than an old dog, it is best to teach children when they are young. Your training becomes ingrained in who they are. They don't develop lifelong habits that they need to break. It becomes a joy to you rather than a struggle.

Can you train older children? *Yes. You. Can.* It takes a bit more creativity and courage, but it's the same concept.

An example of a well-trained teenager:

Your parents come over for a visit. Your seventeen-year-old son welcomes them in and helps your mother into a seat. Your son sits with your parents while you are finishing supper. He asks them about their work, friends, and hobbies. He is genuinely interested. After supper, he eagerly helps clean up the dishes. He asks to be excused when he is done eating to finish his homework.

What kind of training led up to this dreamy child?

>*He welcomes them in.* You might have practiced with him (in a goofy way) to invite people into the home. Maybe you had him write an article on hospitality for school.

>*He sits with parents while you're finishing supper and has an excellent conversation:* You may have been practicing general social skills such as listening, asking questions, using body language to show enthusiasm, and complimenting him for doing it well. You may have mentioned to him before guests arrived how vital conversation is with your parents.

>*He eagerly helps with the dishes.* He practices cleaning up like a champ. He knows his way around the kitchen because he does it every day. He knows what his responsibilities are. Cleaning up is everyday life for him.

>*He asks to be excused:* You practice not allowing him to walk away. This is a big one in my family. Nothing drives me crazier than having to keep calling my kids for attention. By practicing regularly, he automatically asks you if he can be excused.

It isn't hard, but it is done on purpose by you. It can all be done. You have to decide what is essential in your family and create opportunities for your children to practice it. Create lots and lots and lots of opportunities. If your child bombs something in public, it's okay. Just make a note that there are things that need practicing.

Children can only do what they learn. What better way to prepare them than setting up practicing events?

Parenting with training takes practice. Give yourself some grace if this is the first time that you've ever considered this concept. Start one day at a time. Start one conversation at a time. A great way to start training is to begin to think out loud. At first, it will feel like rambling. After a while, you'll realize that each moment that you spend with your children is a gift of training time. You'll laugh and be filled with joy when your children start repeating your stories or experiences. It's a blessing to know that they are listening.

What kind of things do you think? What sort of things could you say out loud? Let me bring you into my day for a minute.

Today my seven-year-old, Claire, was feeling down. She wanted to have some snuggle time, so we crawled into my bed, and I held her while she told me about her woes. As we laid there, and when I realized her boo-hoo-ness was from being tired, I mentioned it.

She said, "why do I feel this way when I'm tired?" This question allowed me to talk to her about the need for rest in the body. Her exhaustion turned into a science lesson and a learning lesson to stay in bed when tired.

After a few minutes, my five-year-old son came into the room with a 7x10 pan. He asked me if it was a cake pan. I said, "No. This pan is a 7x10 pan, and we make a cake in a 9x13." This simple answer led to a discussion of inches, and measurement, and math questions.

Our thinking aloud not only allows us to train our children in the right behavior, but also teaches them so much about life.

When the book of Deuteronomy was written, God told us the importance of teaching His precepts to our children. It still applies today.

Deuteronomy 6:7 says, "You shall teach them diligently to your children, and shall talk of them when you sit in your house, and when you walk by the way, and when you lie down, and when you rise up" (NKJV).

Basically, at any time, in any situation, doing whatever you could be doing, teach your children. Teach them God's precepts and teach them about life. Teach your children moral values and just talk. The more you talk, the more they get to practice listening.

No Greater Joy

When Jesus began His ministry, the Bible says His mother watched him and "treasured up all these things and pondered them in her heart" (Luke 2:19, NIV).

There is something to be said about a child who grows up and becomes an amazing man or woman. When our children are young, it's hard to imagine them as adults, but I assure you, they will be. There isn't a potion that stops them from growing up.

When your children grow up, do you know who they will be? What have you trained them in? Who have you told them they are? Are they destined for greatness?

We are to be their greatest fan.

When we imagine our children as adults, and we ponder their future, it becomes necessary that we train them. Time won't wait.

When Mary was raising Jesus, I wonder if she told him regularly who He was. Did she tell him the story of the angel that announced her pregnancy? Was she keenly aware of His difference as an obedient child? When He began His ministry, did Mary "treasure these things" because she was surprised? I don't think she was surprised. I believe she treasured these things because she knew that He was wonderful. She knew it *far before* His ministry started.

As mothers, we can have joy in our children while they are young. We need to have joy when they succeed. When they learn from mistakes, we can rejoice just as much as if they hadn't made a mistake. We are to be their greatest fan.

"I have no greater joy than to hear that my children are walking in the truth" (3 John 1:4, NIV).

I want to be the mother that has great joy. I want to hear the amazing things that my children are teaching others. The way that God is using them to change the world. This, my dear sister, starts at home, by training them and believing that they will succeed.

A Choice

When I wrote this section, I was sitting in my children's room while they slept. Sometimes it's easier to sit in there to write than to remind them to get back in bed at nap time. Whenever I sit in their room, they fall to sleep in two minutes flat. I could leave, but it's easier for me to stay focused if I suck it up and stay where I am.

When I lay my children down to nap, I know that they are going to disobey. I know they will try to get up and play with their toys quietly. I will require their obedience, but sometimes, obedience comes more naturally when I set them up to win. Hence, the reason I write in their room.

When we love our children, it's a choice. We want them to do the right thing and make the right choices, but we need to remember that they will utterly fail. It's our job as parents to help our children make the right choices. Sometimes it means sitting in their room at nap time. Sometimes it means only putting three pieces of broccoli on their plate instead of a whole scoop. Sometimes it means going to a friend's house with your daughter. Sometimes it involves a double date with a daughter and her boyfriend. We want to set them up for success.

Sometimes to set up our children for success means that they need to practice (training), but other times, it might mean that *we* are the ones who are doing the work. You need to remember that no one ever *feels* like being a good parent. We need to choose it. We have to *decide* to make hard choices for the benefit of our children. We have to *decide* to set ourselves aside. We have to make choices for the benefit of the entire family. Sometimes we have to choose to say "no" to a good thing because it's not right for the family.

Choosing to train our children takes thought. It takes creativity.

It requires us to make new habits. We need to learn how to have systems to teach our children the proper way to live. We need to set boundaries that we don't want to follow ourselves. Yet, to set up your child for success, it's necessary. Here's an example:

> When my daughters started buying their own clothes, I realized that their opinion of what was pretty was a bit too edgy for my taste. Before I could change their thinking on modest apparel, I had to re-evaluate my own closet. When I re-evaluated, I realized that I dressed edgy myself. My husband likes it, so why not? Well, sister, because your daughters will do it too. If you dress edgy, they will too. If you can look hip and confident in modest apparel, then they will too. Whether it's a different style or the same, modesty is learned and practiced according to how a mother regards it. Modesty was a boundary for my girls that I had to include myself in. I'm a grown woman. If I want to wear a low-cut top, I should be able to, right? Sure. But I'll need to expect that my daughter will do it too. I'm not willing to allow her to dress immodestly, so to set her up for success, I had to choose to change.

Choosing to love our family is a massive effort sometimes. Sometimes, you won't feel like choosing the right thing. But you have to choose it anyway. I speak this to myself as much as I'm speaking it to you. It's easy to get frustrated when I want something a certain way. I'm an adult, so I should finally get to do things my way. Unfortunately, it doesn't work quite like that. The choices that you make need to be for everyone. Not choices for just yourself.

Devices and Screen Time

I can't write a chapter about parenting without giving my convictions on devices and screen time. Because I know that many parents struggle with finding balance in this area, I feel that it is necessary to use Scripture to anchor your thinking of the subject.

Here, you will find an outline of Bible verses and how they apply to our children with current social trends. I hope this is helpful for you as you ponder this subject of great importance.

There's a time for everything.

When we look at Scripture regarding spending our time, we see that it is evident there is a time for everything. God doesn't leave anything out. While the Bible doesn't specify the Internet or devices, we can use our logical sense to interpret Scripture to society's current trends.

One thing that stands out for me is that God explicitly says that we need to be wise, using time carefully. In regards to time spent on a device, we need to think this through. If our children are spending more time on their devices than they are in the real world, there will be some problems.

Let's take a look at the brain viewpoint. Have you ever held onto something very tightly for an extended period? When I do this, my fingers ache when I finally let go. If I hold tight enough, I struggle to open my hand back up for quite a while. This struggle is the same thing that happens to our children's brains. When they are immersed in a screen, it becomes difficult for them to enjoy life without the screen. Their body and mind are stuck on Facebook, a game, or TV. This stuck feeling is similar to my hand—not opening up completely. It's even painful for our children to be apart from their devices.

Should we, as parents, limit our time on a screen with our job? Is it showing our children a bad habit? The Bible emphasizes balance. Moderation is key. I don't believe we should limit our jobs if we are using the internet. By all means, use the tools that God has given you to stay home with your children. I do think that if your job is on a screen, that it might be a good idea to limit extra screen time for pleasure. This will show your children how to practice self-control in this area as well.

Children's developing brains will lose vibrancy if they spend too much screen time that isn't productive. Even if it is productive in regards to learning, there must be a balance. I recommend older children utilize online learning for school. Since I do this in my home, I find it imperative to give the children breaks and be very limited on other screens or device time on school days.

If your children spend too much time on devices, how will you have conversations? How will they learn? How will they hear your wisdom and develop deep relationships?

> Ecclesiastes 3:1, "For everything, there is a season and a time for every matter under heaven" (ESV).

> Ephesians 5:15-17, "Look carefully then how you walk, not as unwise but as wise, making the best use of the time because the days are evil. Therefore do not be foolish, but understand what the will of the Lord is" (ESV).

Doing things with our hands is a priority.

This is an area that I struggle with sometimes. I love to get stuff done with my hands, but if I'm not careful, I do too much thinking and planning and lose sight of just doing the thing. I forget to make my hands a priority.

Think about Pinterest. How many boards do you have? I think that I have seventy-two. Well maybe not that many, but there's more than I want to see there. I tend to obsess at ideas and see all the cool things that people create. I can get utterly lost at looking at creative stuff. When I'm ready to do my project, I'm just tired. Too tired to start. I don't think that's what God intended.

If our children spend too much time on a screen, they will see and hear some excellent ideas, but will not do any of them. We need to teach them to work with their hands. They need to touch things, spend time outside, and create something with their hands. Testing things and thinking things through without google to show them how.

In fact, science has shown that children who have extended sensory (touch, hearing, sight, taste, smell) play prepares them for life ahead. Most sensory play focuses on stimulating with touch. It is essential for brain development because it strengthens sensory related synapses and functions. Synapses in the brain are added or pruned based on life experiences. This is called "Experience Dependent Plasticity/Neuroplasticity."

Neuroplasticity is the brain's ability to rewire the brain. By exposing children to various sensory experiences is necessary for a child to develop. In fact, sensory development is even called "The Critical Period" by professionals.[1]

By teaching your child to touch things with their hands, they will learn and retain more information as they grow. Even adults are this way!

The Bible supports science in regards to touch:

> Ephesians 4:28, "Let the thief no longer steal, but rather let him labor, doing honest work <u>with his own hands</u>, so that he may have something to share with anyone in need" (ESV, emphasis added).

> James 1:22, "But be <u>doers of the word</u>, and not hearers only, deceiving yourselves" (ESV, emphasis added).

> Proverbs 10:4, "A slack hand causes poverty, but the <u>hand of the diligent</u> makes the rich" (ESV, emphasis added).

Teach diligently.

Some of the greatest ideas come from boredom.

I think it's easy to turn on the TV when it's raining or the kids are getting after each other. I think it's easy to let them play on the iPad with headphones. I find that when I do this sometimes, I pay greatly for it. Why? Because they need training time.

If my kids are getting after each other during a rainy day, it's not because they need something to do. It's an excellent time to teach them how to contain themselves.

---

1   Rosenzweig MR, Bennett EL. Psychobiology of plasticity: effects of training and experience on brain and behavior. Behavioral Brain Research.

What would be an enjoyable trait of someone in a rainstorm? Someone who likes to sit down and watch the rain? Someone who listens to soft music playing? Someone who appreciates the sound of the raindrops?

When it's raining, do you want to go-go-go? I certainly don't. In fact, when it's raining, I long to lay in bed and listen to the rain while I drift off to sleep. For some reason, our culture has made us think that it's a bad thing if our kids are bored. It's not. Boredom is the beginning of imagination and every innovation that ever existed. Busy lives can keep us from our greatest ideas. In fact, some of the greatest ideas come from boredom.

Maybe when it's raining, I should train my child to sit quietly and enjoy the rain's sound. Let them be bored. It's excellent practice time to sit still and enjoy something that God created.

If we are always stimulating our children with a screen, they lose the ability to think independently. They look for answers on Google when they already know the answer. They become addicted to stimulation and are never content with the beauty that surrounds them.

If you want your children to be competent, they shouldn't use all their free time on a screen. To grow into successful men and women, they need to have experience learning and thinking in their free time. They can't do that if they are stuck on a screen.

> Proverbs 12:24, "The hand of the diligent will rule, while the slothful will be put to forced labor" (ESV).

> 2 Timothy 3:17, "That the man of God may be competent, equipped for every good work" (ESV).

Negative attitudes result from too much stimulation.

This is the big kicker in my home. Thankfully, it's evident to us as parents, and we know what steps to take to correct it. Every once in a while, if my children have spent too much time on devices, I find they have terrible attitudes. They start to feel like a victim and become angry. They argue and look downcast. They make excuses and are forgetful. It becomes a nightmare for me.

When these things happen, I usually just need to have a look at their devices. It could be that they've been playing games too often. Or that they've listened to audiobooks for hours (usually the biggest culprit). Sometimes their music has been continuously playing, and they have had no rest period for their brains. It could be that they had two late nights watching long movies with their daddy. Whatever the case, it almost always points to a device being the issue.

Have you ever read a good book you couldn't put down? I have been known to walk around my house with a book in my hand during those times. I try to minimize my novel reading because of this. Your children have the same obsession with "good things." It could be an audiobook, or a new band they're listening to. It could be a new friend that they're connecting with over text. They could even start a deep godly conversation with a peer. Regardless of the "good" thing, it might not be good if it's too much.

The verses below speak of a sinful heart and eyes causing sin. Not all screen time will cause your child to sin because of content. Devices themselves are not a sin either. I think it's important to know that device stimulation can negatively affect our children's attitudes and emotions. In short, too much stimulation can cause our children to sin. When you see negativities in your children, remove the devices before you do anything else. Chances are, it will solve the problem.

> Matthew 12:34b, "...For the mouth speaks what the heart is full of" (NIV).

> Matthew 5:29, "If your right eye causes you to sin, tear it out and throw it away. For it is better that you lose one of your members than that your whole body is thrown into hell" (NIV).

> 1 John 3:18, "Little children, let us not love in word or talk but in deed and in truth" (ESV).

Social media is also a tough area that needs parental attention. Many parents choose to allow children to be on social media, and careful planning in this area is a must for any parents with teens. I personally do not allow my children on social media unless it is for work, or contacting specific people through my messenger account.

I feel that my children become dissatisfied with their lives when they are seeing all the "things" that others are doing. Since we strive for contentment in our family, it isn't healthy to add in social media.

Since we choose to homeschool our children, we have also asked other homeschoolers in our area what their views of social media are. In our area, it isn't common for homeschooled children to have their own accounts. Because of this, it isn't a surprise for our teens, and we don't have any disagreement issues because of it.

In a home business, sometimes children can be very helpful on social media to help admin groups, or to do market research. If you are seeking work help from your children in this area, just have them do everything under your own name. This will help them to clearly draw the line that Facebook/Instagram/etc. are for work purposes and not pleasure purposes.

Points to Ponder:

What are the ways that I can show true love to my children?

What are the boundaries that I've been neglecting in my home?

What are some new boundaries that I should set?

What are some training ideas that I can implement?

What type of young man/woman do I want my child to become?

What choices can I make to help my children succeed?

What do I feel God is telling me about devices or screen time?

Chapter Two

Structure

Structure is going to make your home life and your work life balanced. Nothing can give you the peace of mind as much as having a time and place for everything. If you create schedules in your day for certain things, you will have peace. If you create spaces in your life free of clutter, you will be quick to succeed in your endeavor.

As I was writing this chapter, God allowed me to have some experiences that formed how this section was written. During this time, I experienced complete structural failure. I hope that my experience and changes that I made will show you how quickly you can implement structure into your life.

My Crazy Work Week

Recently, I had two clients that were sitting in website limbo because of indecisiveness. They wanted to hire me to make amazing websites for them, but were wishy-washy in the process. Each time I was ready to begin, they halted the process and threw in a new concept or idea. These concepts could have been addressed during the site build, but instead we talked, and talked, and talked. I spent countless hours talking with these clients.

Because of the limbo of unfinished projects, and the constant communication, my brain wouldn't let go. I couldn't get my mind off of the projects. No matter what time of day it was, I was thinking of it. I responded to texts and e-mails from my clients during the day or night. I even checked my phone at dinner time. It was insane.

Not only was I struggling to finalize the contracts, but I was letting my children run amok. My children are amazing and find things to keep themselves occupied. However, they began to argue constantly. They would cry at simple disagreements. They watched more TV than I've ever allowed. I was irritable and only half paying attention to conversations. The food that I made was not on time and wasn't very good. I hardly showered, and I looked like a homeless person. My life quickly spiraled into a disaster.

And then….

I had a moment of clarity. I realized that I was writing a book on balance, and I was more unbalanced than I had been in my entire motherhood. Why? Because my desire for completion became more important than real life. I didn't recognize that it was okay if the job didn't get finished immediately. It was okay if the e-mails and texts waited until later. In fact, it was even okay if I never began the projects at all and lost the clients!

> Romans 12:2, "Do not be conformed to this world, but be transformed by the renewal of your mind, that by testing you may discern what the will of God is, what is good and acceptable and perfect" (ESV).

My mind was being worldly. I was obsessing about completing websites, instead of remembering God's will for me. I needed to view my life as a masterpiece, instead of working on one simple detail. God's will for me to be a mother, a wife, a homeschooler and a business owner are all to be done with balance. I had to "renew my mind" by choosing to get back to structure.

> 1 Corinthians 14:40, "But all things should be done decently and in order" (ESV).

I decided to get my life back in order. After the "insane" cycle had gone on for about five days, I decided that it was enough. After waking up extra early to read my Bible, I prayed about what to say to my clients. When I was confident, I wrote them e-mails to explain that I had been putting too much time into their decision-making. I was willing to help them when they were ready, and told them my professional limits on their projects.

Once the e-mails were sent, I resumed my structured routine. I took a walk with my children and enjoyed them. My phone was ignored, and my children played in the mud. We walked, ran, laughed, discussed random science facts, and were together (finally) in body and mind.

Looking back, I realized that I was fearful of walking away from an unfinished project. There was also the fear that I could lose my clients if we didn't get started. When I recognized it as fear, I could see how easy it is to fall into this trap.

2 Timothy 1:7, "For God gave us a spirit not of fear but of power and love and self-control..." (ESV).

When you experience a lack of structure in your life, think about what is causing it.

Maybe you find that clutter is the most significant aspect of your life without structure. Is it possible that you are fearful of throwing things away?

When you experience a lack of structure in your life, think about what is causing it.

Perhaps you find that time management in business (as in my case) is a struggle to be structured. Is it possible that you are fearful of losing business?

Hiring people can be a daunting process because there may be fear about choosing the wrong person to work for you. Yet, without the help, you can't stay structured in your day. An aversion to hiring people could be holding you back from gaining time.

Maybe you aren't ready to make a meal plan. Perhaps you are fearful that you won't stick to it?

After I sent the e-mails to my clients, they were understanding. When we did communicate during the set hours of my workday, it was quick and clearly spoken. I did lose these clients, but the peace was worth it. If I had continued in the direction that I was, I wouldn't be true to myself and my goals.

If you can reach past your fears and decide to live within boundaries that you set (a.k.a., structure), you will succeed. Your life will also be balanced.

Time

The Bible has a lot to say about time. If we are looking through the lens of structure, we can apply this verse in Ephesians.

> Ephesians 5:15a, "Look carefully then how you walk, not as unwise but as wise, making the best use of the time…" (ESV).

This verse tells us that if we use wisdom in our day, we should be making the best use of our time. In short, don't waste time. What are the ways that you misspend time on a typical day? Let's see if we can save time in these areas.

Social Surfing

This is a big one for many moms. Whether it's Facebook or Pinterest, our focus is not on essential things. If you must do social surfing, choose to have a set time in your day for this. Maybe it's after dinner, or perhaps it's only on Saturday afternoons. Whatever the time, please try not to open social media during the day unless it's part of your job.

Primping All Morning

If you are a homeschooling mother, you probably threw primping out a long time ago. However, if you tend to shower and spend an hour in the bathroom each morning, consider showering at night. You may find that an extra hour in the morning saves you an incredible amount of time. Have you tried dry shampoo? It's a game-changer for mornings!

Cleaning Up Clutter

Many parents and business owners have a lot of "stuff." Stuff becomes hard to keep organized without a plan. Try to save time by not cleaning up the clutter. Decide to hold it. I'll have more on organizing later in this chapter.

Picking Up After Our Children

If you have big enough children to make a mess, they are big enough to clean up after themselves. If your children know that they cannot have the next meal until their room is clean, you may find that your children are eager to pick up.

Continually Doing the Dishes

There are days that I feel I am always washing dishes. However, if you have children that can take this responsibility, train them! My five-year-old, Elijah, does a fantastic job cleaning the dishes. He also puts the dishes away in the dishwasher and loads it back up. He still needs some coaching, but overall, Elijah is becoming a dish ninja.

Another way that you can save dishes is by merely dusting them off or rinsing them off. What I mean is, when I use a measuring cup, I rarely wash it after. I just put it back into the drawer unless it was something wet or gooey. It's the same thing with measuring spoons. I'll also re-use our egg pan from breakfast to make lunch. It's only been sitting for a short time, and it saves me precious time.

Recognize the Quality of Teaching

If I did the dishes, I would do it way faster than Elijah. How does it save me time when he's washing? When Elijah does the dishes, I know that it's going to take him nearly an hour. That hour is excellent teaching time for him to stay on task, work efficiently, pay attention to detail, and follow directions. I'm never frustrated with him when he does the dishes because he is getting a chore done while being trained. By recognizing what you are teaching your children, it saves time in your mind. You would have to do the dishes and think up a training exercise otherwise. Win-Win!

Let Your Husband Help You

Many women decide to do things that their husbands said they would do. These women feel that they will never get their projects done if they wait. That may be true. Especially if you have trained your husband to expect you to do everything you've asked him. However, letting your husband do the project himself allows you to think about other things. It saves you time and gives you brain space.

We recognized that there are many ways that we can save time. You probably have some ideas of your own that I didn't include here. That's excellent! Brainstorming ways to save time in your life will be beneficial.

Your children need organization.

Proverbs 13:4, "The soul of the sluggard craves and gets nothing, while the soul of the diligent is richly supplied" (ESV).

You must be diligent about sticking to your schedule. If you decide that it's work time from 2–5 p.m., stick with it. Perhaps school is done from 8 a.m.–12 p.m. Be prepared each day. Set structured times for things in your life, and you will find that you can accomplish all of it. Proverbs 13:4 is clear; we will be richly supplied if we are diligent. So be diligent in your time, become richly supplied in your time.

Organizing

Do you ever get frustrated when you can't find something? What about a tool that you need to use, or a specific book? If I ever struggle to find something, I know that it's time to do some cleaning. More important than locating needed items, organizing saves time because you'll stop looking for things.

Your children need organization. Without anyone teaching them, they can somehow be incredibly messy. They destroy their bedrooms, find the silliest places to stuff things, and even become disheveled. However, just because they have tendencies to be messy doesn't mean they cannot be organized. When you give your children skills to organize (by practicing), they will learn to succeed in their lives. You will also succeed in avoiding needless picking up and cleaning throughout the day.

To begin organizing, you just need to start. Start today. Look at a place in your home or office that needs to be organized. Think about what you can do to tidy up that space, and just do it! It doesn't have to be an expensive "Martha Stewart" kind of organization. You can go to the dollar store and get bins for $1 to completely change how you put things away. In fact, for many years, I organized my home with spray-painted diaper boxes. You can organize anything; you just need to give things a place. Try to organize one area of your home once per week. Although small, this tiny habit will produce excellent results in making your home more productive.

If you live in a small home, start your organization by hanging things on your walls. If you can't put stuff on the floor, stack them up. Hooks and shelves will become your friends. Give things a place, and organize your life. If you cannot find a place for something, determine if it is essential to keep. Have you used it in a year? Will you use it in two months? If you can only say "maybe," then you probably can live without it. Send it off to a thrift store and gain space.

If you have teenagers in the home, asking them to organize or help you make an organization plan (as in an entire closet) is helpful and a great teaching tool. Teens are almost adults and are incredibly smart. Give them opportunities to evaluate organizational projects themselves. Even younger children can be part of the fun of organizing. Test them; they might surprise you with their skills.

Daily Lists

For most of my life, I have been a list person. My mother would write lists of chores for me as a child, and I took the habit to heart. After I became a mother myself, I became a little obsessed with lists. I had lists of lists and spent most of my time writing out things to be done. However, I spent too much time writing and not enough time doing. When I was finally able to spend time accomplishing things on my list, I couldn't find them. They were everywhere.

About four years ago, I read about "Bullet Journaling." The concept was utterly foreign to me and a little too intense. However, I loved the simple idea of using one notebook/journal at a time. In one notebook, I could keep…

- *Meal lists*
- *Grocery list*
- *To-do lists*
- *Notes for the day*
- *Notes for the kids*
- *School ideas*
- *Work ideas*
- *Future plans*
- *Remodeling plans*
- *Budgets*
- *Christmas gift lists*
- *Birthday lists*

And a whole lot more. Since then, I've kept the concept, but I've adapted a few other tools that I'd like to share with you.

Meal List on the Fridge

Okay, I realize that this section speaks for itself. However, I just wanted to point out why I keep my meal list on the fridge. You see, my older children help with meal times. I love knowing that at any time, they can see what is for breakfast or lunch. If they take the time to make their own, I ask that they also make it for everyone else. It's super helpful.

I also keep it on the fridge because I'll often take my meal list with me from room to room. If I leave it in my bedroom, it's not convenient to pull out dinner items from the fridge.

I keep my meal list on notebook paper and clip it up with a magnetic clip. This works well because I keep all of my previous meal plans in a binder. I like to look at them from time to time for fresh ideas of meals that I forgot.

Grocery List

I don't keep my grocery list in my notebook anymore. Instead, I downloaded a Grocery Pick-up App on my phone and use their grocery pick-up service. Many grocery stores offer grocery pick-up now, so take advantage of this service. Grocery pick-up saves time, and it also allows you to have your grocery list within easy reach at any time. Doing grocery pick-up has significantly reduced my grocery budget because I only buy what I need. It also helps me to keep my children in tow with an educational audiobook playing. We love to take grocery trips as a family now!

The Calendar

My calendars have been the source of sanity in my life. I regard them for each thing that I do. I cannot possibly remember everything that I must do without one. I even prefer to keep my previous calendars to look back on them from time to time.

After our web business became busier, I realized that I needed to combine my work schedule, home schedule, and school schedule. It has been a fantastic way to keep track of our lives.

I use Google Calendar and keep the app on my phone and computer. My husband also has access to it, and we can see our full schedule at any time. Because my family would plan things for each moment, I purposefully write "NO PLANS" on days that I want to keep open.

If you want to achieve balance in your life, you need to bring it all together. Your school days need to be written on each day. Any field trips or school-related activities need to be written in. If your children have jobs, write them in as well. Are you taking a day off? Write it in the calendar with the reason you're taking it off. This will help to intentionally keep the day what it was intended for.

Scheduling

My dear friend, Anne, has been a mother for twenty-two years. She has homeschooled five children, of whom two have graduated already. She has gone through multiple life phases and speaks with much wisdom. When her children were young, she incorporated sit time and a plethora of other tips that I have described in this book. In fact, much of my learning has been through her teaching. As her children grew, Anne pulled away from her rigid schedule and became more free-spirited.

Anne continues to homeschool three children and owns a successful beauty business. She develops amazing formulas that nourish and heal the skin. My friend loves to pour her energy into family activities and the creative aspects of her business. However, she hasn't managed to spend as much time in her specialty as she'd like. Recently Anne told me about her new passion…

While at a wedding, she grabbed me and whispered in my ear, "You'll never believe what I'm doing these days." She had a mischievous look about her as she raised her eyebrows, waiting for my response.

I couldn't read her expression, so I asked, "What is it?" What could it possibly be? I have known Anne for years, and they are always doing something fun. I contemplated what exciting things she could be planning.

"I'm putting intense structure into our schedule. It's going amazing!" She laughed as she said it. She knew I was aware of her "schedule-less" tendencies as her children grew. We had discussions about scheduling before, and this was a huge deal.

I laughed with her and asked, "Really? Why is it amazing?" I couldn't wait to hear how she was doing it.

"Oh, you know. I'm going to bed on time and waking up early to read my Bible. I've been in bed about 10:00 each night! I'm getting so much done, even before lunch. I feel like myself again!"

As she spoke, her eyes sparkled with enthusiasm. I laughed again at the silliness of our conversation. I am probably the only person in the world who is excited about going to bed early. I couldn't be happier for her.

Anne continued, "My kids aren't even sure what to do. They can't believe I'm requiring them to start school at 8 in the morning!" She laughed again, "This is going to be so good for them."

My sweet friend, Anne. My friend, who never turns down a party, get together, bonfire, or late-night conversation. She sleeps in, stays out late, and eats dinner at 10 p.m. Yet, here she was, coming back to what truly works for her family and business. She realized that there are ramifications to stepping outside of structure. I was so blessed that she told me about her plan. She has it right! After multiple years of less structure, she is making a change—what a beautiful example for us to admire.

There is nothing that you can't accomplish with effort.

As I threw my head back in laughter, I realized that this would be an incredible encouragement to many women. Anne's courage to transform back into an organized lifestyle is inspiring for us all. Like Anne, there is nothing that you can't accomplish with effort. If you can't find time to work your business, get up early. If you struggle to wake up on time, then go to bed at a decent hour. If you're struggling to get your children's school done, set the schedule. They learn from your example. Remember what I said in the parenting chapter… "Your children will do what you do."

Set your schedule to allow for "playtime," but keep it minimal compared to your structured time. If you want your children to be successful in time management, then it's time you roll up your sleeves and take control of your time. If you want your children to finish school before they're twenty-five, they need to take school as seriously as a job. This means waking up and getting it done.

Anne saw the benefit of scheduling her homeschool and her business time. She lived without adhering to a schedule for a long time and realized that it wasn't worth it. To move ahead, she took steps forward, even if they were small. Going to bed on time is a small step toward growing her business, but it is a step nonetheless.

Consistency

When you begin a lifestyle of structure, the key to success is consistency. You can start any habit, but you must do it consistently to make it stick. If you'd like to learn more about habits, please read one of my favorite books, *Atomic Habits* by James Clear.

If you want to be consistent with a habit, you have to make your habit realistic. If you're going to work ten hours a day, it's not a realistic goal. It's also not practical for you to set hours where you only work for twenty minutes at a time. A realistic goal for homeschool and a working schedule is setting up "chunks" of time.

The typical brain takes approximately fifteen minutes to become engrossed in an activity. If interrupted by an outside source, it takes equally as long to get back into focus. This means that you don't really begin to move forward with school or business until you've been at it for fifteen minutes or longer.

On the flip side, if a person desires to focus for too long, they can become unproductive at their task. Your focus allowance truly depends on your personality. For instance, I work best if I have three- (or more) hour periods to focus on something. However, any more than five hours makes my brain feel like mush. I can work in two-hour periods; however, I become frustrated that I can't get much accomplished in only two hours. Having three- to five-hour chunks to work is excellent for me to feel accomplished and motivated for the next work session.

On the other hand, my husband prefers to work for extended periods (six or more hours), but he loses steam at eight hours.

There are not likely to be many five-hour periods in a week if you are a mother, homeschooler, and business owner. However, if you can plan weeks to include at least one five-hour chunk, more can be accomplished than eight one-hour time periods. Weekends are a great time to make this happen. Getting help from a friend or grandparents is also helpful during the week. If you can achieve this extra time, make sure that you have a written plan ahead of time. This will help you to get as much done during your workday as possible.

Finally, when you are contemplating a schedule, remember that your family also needs quality time. If you are spending hours being creative for your business, and hours focused on school, you should also spend focused time on your precious family. This includes any type of quality time that you can do together. Make it count, whether eating with a conversation, taking walks, playing games, or reading Scripture together. Your family time is more important than any other time in your life.

Example Schedule

So what does a structured schedule look like? I know you're wondering how to fit it all in, so I wanted to write out a typical schedule that I work with. In our family, we have two "sets" of children. One set is the Bigs (ages fifteen and sixteen), and the other "set" are the Littles (ages three, five, and seven). I must take account of all of my children's needs during the day. Please feel free to modify my example to fit your own parenting and children's needs.

6:00 a.m.

This is my time. I sip my coffee, read my Bible, and think. I have two notebooks with me; one is my "prayer" journal, and the other is my regular journal. I turn my regular journal to a new page and use it as a "thinking" page. I believe that I am most creative and clear-headed at this time of day. My Bible reading and prayer will often spur some thoughts about business, so I want to have a separate place to write them down. This has proved to be the most valuable part of my day. I also like to write a small list of my plans for the day during this time. I discussed this at length in the "Spiritual Health" chapter.

7:00 a.m.

Wake-up for the Bigs. This is my Bigs' time to get up. They stay in their room or bathroom. They have reading time to themselves, and also get ready for the day. This is also when I get myself prepared for the day and do anything that I need to do before little feet hit the ground.

8:00 a.m.

Wake-up for the Littles. This is when the Littles come out of their rooms. They brush their teeth, start their morning chores, and everyone gathers for breakfast. During breakfast, we discuss the day's events and anything else that we need to have a family discussion about. Remember how I told you about the light-up clock? This clock is exactly how I taught my young children to stay in their beds until eight.

8:30–9:00 a.m.

Starting the day. This is when we have family Bible reading or discussion of anything pressing. We typically will read one chapter together, discuss, pray, and go on our way.

After Bible time, my husband works, my Bigs begin a load of laundry, clean up breakfast dishes, feed the animals, and go do school (usually in their room or basement), and my littles are ready to start their day.

During this time, we prepare food for the day. Lunch items like rice or beans are perfect for cooking early. Dinner items like meats or soups are easily made at this time as well.

The Littles finish unloading the dishwasher, gather remaining laundry, and water our plants. This is not playtime, and the children know that when they are done with their chores, we begin our school day. My littles all have their own duties to do, and they do them each day.

10:00–10:30 a.m.

Bible lessons. This is when we begin our school day with the Littles. We start by sitting down in the living room and doing our Bible lesson. Bible is always first because it's the most important. If you get nothing else done in your day, Bible class is the one you should aim for. Because we are doing Bible class on video, it gives me time to shower or finish any dinner plans, garden picking, cleaning, or a quick phone call. It's also a great time to get some sit-ups and push-ups in.

11:00 a.m.

General school time. Once the Bible lesson is over, we move on to our remaining subjects. I like to do reading lessons with my two smallest children, while the third does schoolwork independently. When reading is finished, we work on other bookwork until lunchtime.

12:00 p.m.

Lunch time. Everyone meets for lunch. We discuss our school and anything else that we can laugh about. After lunch, the Bigs do some clean-up while the littles play outside, or have Lego® time on rainy days. Rainy days are also a great time to play educational computer games for computer learning. I prefer this to be free-play time for my Littles.

1:00–3:00 p.m.

Rest time for the two littlest, school time for middle, and school time for Bigs. This is also the time that I use for my business. In fact, I try to work from 1–5 twice per week if I can plan ahead. My children know that they cannot interrupt me. If the school gets finished, the remainder of the rest time is for reading only. If the Bigs finish school during this time, they do their chores, music practice, or exercise.

I also like to use this time to take a thirty-minute walk a couple of times a week. It's easy to do some more in-depth learning for your business while you walk on the treadmill. You may also have client phone calls while you are walking. Utilize time, sister.

3:00 p.m.

Snack time. Everyone always wakes up and comes running for snack time. I'll typically have my Bigs make a snack for my Littles, but if you don't have Bigs of your own, it would be easy to have string cheese and an apple on hand. After snack time, we have a history or literature lesson. I like to listen to our history lesson on audio to get some sit time in for the children. This also allows me to finish whatever business project I was working on before snack.

4:00 p.m.

Errand time. If we are going to go to the library or the grocery store, this is the time of day that I prefer to do it. If I'm not doing errands, the children have free play time while I do other things that need to get done. I do things like meal planning, garden tending, cleaning, etc. This is also a great time of day to connect with the older children, give them jobs to do with the business, or have a phone call with a friend. The children can also play computer games or do a typing lesson at this time. We greatly enjoy using YouTube channels for art learning and extra science lessons.

If I have a babysitter or grandparent that is planning to spend time with my children while I work, this is the time that I plan it. I will also often use this opportunity for busy boxes for my Littles. I'll talk more about this later.

6:00 p.m.

Dinner time. We all convene for dinner at this time. After dinner, we clean up and usually do something together, whether it is a game or a movie. Sometimes we go for walks, and sometimes we even exercise together. If the Bigs have youth group, this is when they would leave to do that. My husband and I love to communicate during this time, and we have two hours of just being together as a family without distraction.

8:00pm

Bed time. This is when the Littles go to bed. I'll try to get some work done after they go to sleep. I'm usually in bed sleeping by 9:30–10:00 p.m. Sometimes you'll find me up until 11 p.m. though when I'm finishing a project.

9:00 p.m.

Curfew for Bigs. Just thought I'd mention it.

This schedule is fantastic for a Monday–Friday routine. It allows about fifteen to twenty-five hours' worth of work per week. Any grandma time or weekend time is a bonus for work. If you have a co-op or playgroup that your children get to attend, use that time for action! If you have plans in the morning for your children to have a playdate, use this time. You'll get tasks done while they play, and you can swap your school to the afternoon.

Fifteen to twenty-five hours might not be enough work time for you during the week. Sometimes I also have that dilemma. During these times, it's perfectly acceptable to work for an entire day once per week. Older children can do school without your help. However, younger children need something to do. During these days, I will ask a grandparent or a friend to spend time with the small children for one day per week (I usually do Fridays). If you are comfortable with a daycare setting, this is also an option, but my least favorite.

You can do this, mama. It is totally possible to run a business and homeschool your children.

Young Children Sit Time

You've seen me describe "Sit Time" in a couple places by now. This section is dedicated to explaining how this is done. Children who can sit on their own, all the way to fourth-grade, love sit time. It takes practice, but once it is part of your routine, you will be thankful that you put forth the effort. However, sit time is best accepted by your children if you have structure in place.

Sit time is a scheduled time that children will sit in one place and not move away from the designated location. They will be quiet and content in whatever activity (or no activity) that you give them. Sit time allows children to be quite comfortable sitting still. It gives them the practice to be quiet and to listen to your instructions. By providing your children the gift of sit time, you are also setting them up for success in school, church, and even grandma's house. If your children can learn how to be still and quiet, you will give them a gift...as well as to yourself.

Sit time should always be done by having the children sit in the same place. This will allow them to be content and know what to expect. If you lay a blanket on the floor, they must use the same blanket each time. If you use the table, have them sit in the same spot every time. If sit time is on their bed, make sure that each sit time is done there.

When you begin to practice sit time with little ones, you must start at a low time. Even five minutes is a lot for some toddlers. I typically teach my children to sit up to one hour, so you must have them go potty before beginning sit time. I chose one hour because that is approximately how long a church service will be. For them to sit contentedly with me in church, they must practice sitting at home.

When I have sit time for my children, I always use a timer. This way, they know it will end. In fact, the dollar store's cheap timers work great because they can visually see the progress. If you do not use a timer, your children believe that whining or being noisy will allow them to get up. However, the timer becomes the authority when it is used.

I also have specific things for them to do during sit time. This is why they love sitting. I have multiple containers filled with dollar store items that they are allowed to play with and study. These are their "busy boxes." I never let my children decide which container they want because they will inevitably fight over them. Instead, I choose for them. I love to mix and match things in these boxes so that they can get creative. I may add buttons with matchbox cars and a piece of modeling clay. Or beads with the small animals and a part of cardstock. You cannot go wrong in this area. However, many homeschool mamas make busy boxes for you. You can purchase them premade, and it's one less thing to think about.

Join our community on Facebook for some great resources. www. Facebook.com/groups/HomeschoolDirectory

A small sample of ideas for busy boxes:

- *Legos*
- *Small animals*
- *Small shiny stones*
- *Buttons*
- *New markers and a coloring pad*
- *Modeling clay (I use a cookie sheet with this one)*
- *Beads (also use a cookie sheet)*
- *Cardstock and colored pencils*
- *Puzzles (by age group)*
- *Blocks for building*
- *Matchbox cars*
- *Dollar store toys (quiet ones)*

If you have been practicing sit time and a school schedule for a while, try to get work done during the children's school time. It's also possible to allow children to have a "busy box combine party." This is when you let them combine busy boxes and play to their hearts' content. Plan this after you've already bought new supplies for your busy boxes. Doing a "busy box combine" will give you two hours minimum for some focused work time. Make sure to tell the children that this is the last time they will have the opportunity to play with these toys. Afterward, I literally get rid of them. You might save a few things, but after being stuck in clay, and drawn on, just begin anew.

Another thing that I like to do for sit time is to use this time for learning. YouTube has some fantastic and free science lessons. These videos stimulate children's brains and can be integrated into school. You'll love how your children play after learning some new fun facts.

Another thing that I like to use for sit time are "Busy Books." This is simply a wide range of books that have great pictures to look at. When we go to the library, I like to pick out a pile of books for this purpose. I never let the children see the books until they have sit time with busy books. Looking through these books carefully and thoroughly for an hour is a fantastic thing for them to practice. It's always fresh material to spike their interest. Sometimes I will give them some tracing paper so that they can trace out of the books. Definitely try this idea. It's so fun!

My last piece of sit time can be described quite simply: Do nothing.

Sometimes, (not often), allow your children to sit still doing nothing. This will enable them to appreciate sit time with the busy boxes. It will also allow them to experience sitting for long periods (like church) without something to entertain them. Remember what I explained in the parenting chapter—your children will do what they practice. If they can sit still for an hour doing nothing, then they can sit still for an hour in church.

Points to Ponder:

When do you experience moments like "my crazy week"?

What are ways that you might waste time?

Is fear causing lack of structure in my life? Where?

What areas can I organize in my home or office?

What lists could I combine?

What calendars and schedules could I combine?

Are there areas of my life that I can put structure?

What would be an ideal working time-chunk for me?

Chapter Three

Adult Relationships

If you're going to be successful with all the things you want to accomplish, such as homeschooling, being a good mother, and running a business, you're going to need to focus some on your adult relationships. Let's look at a few things you can do to grow and encourage your relationships and how it will affect your overall balance. This section aims to get a closer look at how relationships must be successful in order to gain momentum in parenting, homeschooling, and business ownership.

Husband

While I'd love to share my greatest experiences with you about my marriage, I will save that for a different book. In this section, let's take a look at Scripture and what it says about our marriage and balance. Your husband needs to be your closest friend and confidant. It's imperative that your relationship with your husband comes before homeschool and business; however, I'd like you to see how you can encourage your husband to support your homeschool your business endeavors.

Trust.

Trust is king in marriage. When you have trust between yourself and your husband, it can impact everything in your life.

Proverbs 31:11 says, "The heart of her husband safely trusts her; So he will have no lack of gain" (NKJV).

Your husband needs to be able to trust you. If you are going to be a homeschooling mother and rocking a business, he needs to know that you're going to follow through on your commitments to him. In fact, if you are the main parent who is homeschooling, trust is imperative between you.

When I go through crazy periods of remodeling in my home, my husband loves the outcome. Still, he isn't excited about the prospect. Why? Because I tend to forget about his needs. I stay up late to work instead of spending time with him. I also end up sleeping in or getting my day started before making breakfast (making his breakfast is our routine). If I upset our routines, he feels unstable. Our trust isn't "broken," but he doesn't feel sure-footed. Your husband needs to know that he can trust you to keep a stable relationship with him while beginning new chapters in your life.

Here are a few examples of ways that you can nurture trust in your relationship with your husband:

Protecting secrets.

If you want your husband to trust you, you need to keep the things he says to you to yourself. Anything that he might be sensitive about, don't bring up to others. If your husband suspects that you are discussing his failures or less desirable qualities to others, there will be a lack of trust in your relationship. On the flip side of protecting secrets, do not keep secrets from your husband. In regards to homeschool, be completely open with him about progress or frustrations with school. You might be embarrassed or not want to bother him with minor details, but our husbands truly care about children's schooling

I also find that my husband prefers to know about many business decisions that I wouldn't necessarily tell him about. Make sure that you have a clear understanding of what is okay to do without his knowledge in business.

Ask his advice first.

If you want your husband to be your best friend and to trust you, you need to ask his advice before asking others. If your husband knows that you trust his opinions, he will trust the choices that you make when he's not around.

This includes asking for advice with your homeschool and business.

Give him the details.

When you have decisions that you need to make, before asking for your husband's advice, get all the details. By gathering details, you can build your plan. Your husband will trust your choices when you lay it all out before him. If you want your husband to trust your curriculum choices or business decisions, you must present all the options and details to him so that he knows you've chosen wisely. You may even ask him for his advice, but tell him what you'd choose based on your research. In the future, if your husband isn't available to help make a decision, he will trust that you'll make a thorough choice. A way that I have experienced this in homeschool is by getting details to new curriculums before asking my husband's opinions.

In business, I have researched and interviewed freelancers and contractors before getting his input. My husband appreciates my approach in this because he doesn't need to search for information. I already have all the details ready for him to see.

Strive to fulfill his expectations.

My husband is particularly sensitive to smells. When he enters a room, he will often smell something that no one else can. Sometimes he asks me to wash the floor or find the smell (even if I don't think it exists). By striving to fulfill his expectations, I wash the floor, remove the furniture covers, and clean anything that could produce the smell. When he sees that I take his request seriously, he trusts that I will work in his best interest. If I don't have time in my day to do the request, I tell him. I don't want him to expect that I will fix the smell if I can't meet that expectation.

You can do this yourself. It might not be as big of a job as washing the floor, but make sure that you meet his expectations even if it is. If you can't meet the request, make sure that he knows. You don't want him to think you are ignoring his needs. Nothing can make a man feel less willing to help you than if he thinks you ignore his desires.

In homeschool and business, this tip is extremely important

because he is trusting you to be the leader in important areas of your life. By fulfilling his expectations, and taking his requests seriously, even in small things, he knows that you will make educated and good decisions if he isn't around.

Be kind.

This might seem like an obvious trait for a marriage. Many women don't realize what kindness means to their husbands. When you are purposefully kind, make sure that you smile. Make sure to give him undivided attention when he speaks. Be genuinely interested in his interests. Show him that you care about him by being kind.

When you are kind to your husband, he trusts that you will also be thoughtful in his absence. When you are kind to him, he will not become jealous of your kindness toward your children or your clients. However, if you choose to be unkind to your husband, he will assume that others drain all of your energy and "goodness," making him unlikely to be supportive of your endeavors.

Encourage him.

When was the last time that you told your husband, "good job"? Even if it is a mindless task, your husband needs encouragement. Does he work in a stressful environment? Does he keep his head level when others around him lose theirs? Does he do monotonous jobs for you or your family? That man needs encouragement.

> 1 Thessalonians 5:11 says, "Therefore encourage one another and build one another up..." (NIV).

This verse was talking about the members of the church. If God thinks it's important enough for church members to encourage each other, I think it's likely that he wants the wife to encourage her husband.

When you encourage your husband, whether it's vocally or as an act of kindness, your husband will trust that you have his best interest in mind. He will know that you genuinely care about what he cares about.

By encouraging your husband, you can bet that he will also start to encourage you. Sometimes we need our husband's to notice things about school, or our business. If we are noticing and enjoying him, he is apt to notice what you are doing as well.

Don't sweat the small stuff.

As I'm sure you are aware, living with another human being can be a challenge. Living with a man can be more of a challenge because they don't think how we think. They can be messy, inattentive, loud, and challenging of our ideas. However, when you genuinely want to foster a balanced marriage, you need to decide to let go of the small stuff. Here's a silly example:

> Whether I'm hot or cold, I really dislike a fan blowing on me. It makes my skin itch and makes me feel clammy, cold, and frustrated. At night time, I don't want air blowing on me at all. My husband, on the other hand, loves the fan. He would have three fans running in our bedroom if he could. He would put one fan in the window, one the ceiling, and one the floor. If they were all aimed at him, he'd be in his glory. This can make sleeping next to him a bit difficult because of my irritation with the fan. I whined about the fan for nearly a decade before I decided that I would let go of my fan struggle. It wasn't worth it. I just decided to embrace the fan. Even though I didn't like it, I pretended that I did. I practiced this pretending until I actually enjoyed it blowing on me. I know it sounds crazy, and to some, it might not be "true to yourself." However, the fight was over. I decided to be on the same team as my husband about a petty fan disagreement.

My sweetheart is always available for my children's questions. Sometimes this means that he gets to his office later than I expected him to on school days. This usually means that we are starting school later than I hoped. I used to be really aggravated at his "lack of school consideration." However, once I realized the preciousness of why he was running late, I decided to be thankful for his attentiveness to the children instead of irritation.

What about irritating things that might disrupt your homeschool or work day? Don't sweat these things. If your husband interrupts you, or distracts the children, decide not to be bothered.

I encourage you sister: let go of the small stuff. You'll become embittered to your husband if you don't let it go. With bitterness comes stress. With stress comes the inability to reach your goals. So turn and kiss your sweetie.

Having a large family and running a business has definitely caused my husband and I to become closer in a plethora of ways. However, there was a time when our marriage was very difficult. We used to disagree on nearly everything regarding parenting, and even business. Constant disagreement was a large strain on our marriage. Foods that the children ate, how often we should incorporate nap time, required hours to work, financial responsibilities, among other things became extremely difficult to find common ground on.

I want to encourage you: you can work through whatever situation that you feel there is disagreement in. After being married and living in relational chaos, my husband and I finally figured it out. We need to listen to each other. Sounds funny right? Listening actually doesn't come naturally to many people. I am one of those. It takes effort to even consider listening sometimes.

The first few years of our marriage, we both suffered from selfishness that wouldn't allow us to really grasp each other's thoughts or ideas. Instead of understanding his point of view, I used to be hardheaded and not give his opinion a second thought. This would cause anger and frustration of not being heard. To someone with a selfish mindset, it is almost a sacrifice to lay down a personal conviction (or opinion) for the sake of listening. I know this to be true of myself in our early marriage.

Do you ever feel like the expert of a certain topic? It's easy to assume that role when you give something careful attention, thought, and time. Things like parenting babies, or Work-at-Home Mom groups aren't exactly husband-ish conversation topics. Yet sometimes, a husband wants to discuss them.

Whether you are an expert at something or not, it is imperative to listen to your husband's advice and thoughts. Sometimes we think that we have all the answers ourselves, and without the willingness to listen to your spouse, you'll never build a lasting, selfless relationship.

When your husband tells you an opinion or idea, do you really listen? Try to really contemplate his idea as if it were your own. This is hard to accomplish in the beginning, but it will eventually come naturally. You'll find that listening will be worth the effort and your marriage will become grounded in new ways.

As you go about your life and ponder this chapter, please consider ways to listen to your husband. Instead of being irritated at irrational expectations or ideas, really ponder and consider them. Talk them through with your husband. If you listen to him, you will find that he also becomes willing to listen to you. It takes ONE person to start the listening process in a relationship. I encourage you to be the first one.

Deep Circle

When it comes to relationships with friends or extended family (such as cousins or in-laws), we have some important choices to make. It feels good to have multiple "friends." However, if you have more than four friendships at once, you can't possibly give them much of a relationship while building a home business and homeschooling.

When our teens were younger, about twenty-five kids got together for church, youth group, Christian dances, swimming parties, homeschool events, and meetings for hangouts. Because of our children's diverse ages, and because of our schedule, it wasn't a possibility very often to attend these get-togethers. The impossibility to go to events while being with the group would frustrate our young teens.

We realized they didn't want to be with "a" friend—our teenagers didn't have deep relationships with any of the kids in the group. Their frustrations were not that they couldn't go to all the events, but that they didn't have individual friendships. Once we discovered that our teens needed to develop individual friendships instead of "group" friendships, they were content to skip the group events. They needed to focus on individual relationships. Now they are blossoming with excellent relationships with a few close friends. This is also something that many of us mothers need in our lives as well.

A wise, dear friend of mine told me once, "There are many things you could do, but not the time for them all. You must choose carefully."

Relationships must be chosen carefully. This takes effort and decisions on your part. Sometimes it's hard to choose between relationships. It can and should be done wisely. When you are homeschooling, choosing our friendships should be done with our entire family in mind. I will expand on this later.

Our extended family ties are extremely important to my family. We have incredible relationships with both sets of our parents and include them in our friendship circle. We also include my sister in nearly everything. She has children the same age as ours, and we have similar values. We genuinely help each other grow, and our relationships are astonishingly deep. Having two sets of parents and my sister's family creates room for only one or two other close relationships. If I try to balance more relationships than that, I will not give them my very best. I will always feel behind, and I won't be able to follow through with commitments.

By including family into our close circle of friends, it allows us to be unhindered with asking for help when we need it. When I need a few uninterrupted hours to work, or a weekend to get a project done, our parents love to have some grandkid time.

If I have a homeschooling event that only requires one child, it's great to send the rest of the children to have a playdate with cousins.

Family tends to be easier to depend on (at least in our case) for last minute visits or extended visiting time when we have a work deadline approaching.

What does a good friendship look like when you choose your friends carefully? It should be beneficial for each of you. You'll be able to support each other in work projects or homeschooling. You'll have similar interests, so having great conversations will be easy and fulfilling. Your children will enjoy each other, and you can help each other by watching each other's children when necessary. A good friendship should consistently build character and learn new things.

One of my favorite things about my close friendships is having a soundboard to discuss deep, spiritual matters. To me, nothing is sweeter than to hear scripture come from the mouth of a friend.

A good friendship is done on purpose. Purposefully choosing to talk, or spend time together is important. Looking for ways to serve each other is imperative—it leads to lasting and deep closeness.

Focus

If you've ever watched a team ice skating competition, you've seen people with intense focus. The skaters train hard and work together under any circumstance. It doesn't matter if someone becomes tired or if there is an illness. No matter what, these professional ice skaters practice together to make a beautifully choreographed routine. When they perform in a competition, they focus on each other, the movements, and hitting each beat in sync. During a competition, it is as if nothing else exists. The result of their focus is a "dance" on ice that is more spectacular than any performance of a single skater. Together, the skaters can do far more stunts and movements than if they were apart.

When you have a friend with the same focus as you, you move farther and better than you would if you were alone. Let's look at some ways that we should share focus with friendships.

Parenting Focus

If you are homeschooling, it's important to socialize your children and give them opportunities for friendships. Just as you will choose carefully for yourself, you want to choose carefully for your children. If you feel encouraged by a friend, but their children are toxic, this may be a relationship that you do not pour into. Whoever is your friend will spill over onto your children.

Whoever you allow into your deeper circle of friendship should have the same parental values as you (or similar). In fact, look for parents that you can learn from. Add these people to the top of your list of friendship possibilities.

Proverbs 13:20 says, "Whoever walks with the wise becomes wise, but the companion of fools will suffer harm" (ESV).

If parenting and homeschooling well are a priority for you, consider parents who are wise in this area. You may feel inferior at first, but surrounding yourself with wisdom will produce wisdom in yourself.

Allow yourself to be open to new homeschooling ideas. Many times friendships among homeschoolers can be a valuable asset to your family. You'll learn multiple new things about homeschooling if your friendship circle is also homeschool focused. I'll touch more on this in the Chapter 9: Homeschool 101.

You may feel inferior at first, but surrounding yourself with wisdom will produce wisdom in yourself.

Choose friendships of people who are good parents. By doing this, you are setting your family up for healthy, balanced relationships. You will trust that your children will be in safe hands if they are with your friends, and your friends will enjoy your children's company as well. By having friends or family with the same parenting mentality as you, you are setting yourself up for success.

Similar Interests

When you develop relationships, these are done easiest if you can find things that you have in common. Maybe it's gardening. Perhaps you both like to travel. You could both be coffee drinkers and want to try out a new brew from time to time. Regardless of the similar interest, try to make it a priority to find things in common. You can use those things to build your relationship initially.

Something that I find important in my relationships is the ability to be friends with someone who has a healthy relationship with her husband. I especially enjoy friendships which allow my husband time to interact with guy friends from time to time. When I am friends with a woman who is in a good marital relationship, my husband also gains a friend.

It's always fun to find people who have similar interests as you do, but don't be alarmed or disheartened if you don't have a lot in common. It's incredibly useful for you to have friends with varying interests as well. You will learn about life and experiences that you didn't have before. Your children will become knowledgeable about things that are different than the typical life that you live. You will have more exposure to people who think differently than you do. This is incredibly important for learning how to communicate with clients or other business owners while building your business.

Learn to appreciate differences in people. Use those opportunities to ask questions and learn more about those differences. Try some of their quirky habits to see if they work for your family. Use those experiences to lead to more laughter and discussion.

If you have friends who are business minded, be open to their business suggestions. Talk them out. Many ideas in my business comes from simple, friendly conversation with people who are close to me.

Spiritual Goals

My friend Michelle is my dearest friend. It's incredible how we fit each other so perfectly. We were truly blessed that God gave us friendship as He has. We are alike in many ways, but we are also very different. She is soft mannered; I tend to be boisterous. She is careful to consider projects, and I blaze a trail with a chainsaw. Michelle loves animals, and I prefer to keep my distance. There are many more things that I could list, but you get the picture. Yet we balance each other and help to encourage each other more than any other friends in our lives. Why? Because our spiritual goals are the same.

Recently, Michelle told me to read a book that changed the way that she was reading Scripture. Of course, I was going to comply, and immediately we had another beautiful connection. We began to read a passage of Scripture and share notes daily—we still do now! She may live three hours away from me, yet our spiritual connection creates a bond that nothing else could.

When you have a friend who can encourage you to dive deeper into your relationship with God, you have a real friend. Having a friend who is not afraid to tell you that you're wrong in an area is a blessing. If you have a friend who is wise and knows your weaknesses, you can be sure to learn.

Seek friendships in which you can build each other up.

> Proverbs 27:17 says, "As iron sharpens iron, so does a man sharpen the countenance of his friend" (NKJV).

Desire a friendship that you can encourage and speak out your faith continually. Listen to advice from each other and ask spiritual opinions. If you don't have a friendship like this, ask the Lord to open your eyes. There may be someone nearby waiting for a relationship with you.

Supportive

My friend Michelle is soft-mannered and careful, so she sees a different perspective than I do. When I can be headstrong and fast-paced, she reminds me of the mistakes that I may make or the things that I may forget. She is supportive of me in projects or tasks because she tends to see the things I do not. In fact, even in the writing of this book, I sought the council of my friend regarding the homeschooling chapter. She encouraged me, but also reminded me of things that I forgot, or was incorrect with. Because she is such a talented teacher of her children, I was able to get support from her regarding school.

Michelle appreciates me just as much as I do her. She continually tells me how she tries to think "like Elizabeth" when she wants to be bold or get something done. I encourage her to take the leap and make her believe in herself. If she makes a mistake, I'm right there to hold the line for her. Above all things, we support each other in wisdom. Because we love each other, I want to always keep her following Truth. She does the same for me.

> Proverbs 13:20 says, "Whoever walks with the wise becomes wise, but the companion of fools suffers harm" (NIV).

You may be different in personality traits, but your weaknesses can be strengthened by a friend. Likewise, you may strengthen a friend in her weakness. Sometimes this is helping with homeschool ideas, business ideas, or simply being an ear to listen while giving godly counsel.

Don't be afraid to get your hands dirty with a friend. Be willing to help them move or clean their garage. Be supportive of her endeavors and ask that she support yours. Even if you are not gifted in an area that she is, help her in the best way possible.

> Ecclesiastes 4:9-12 says, "Two are better than one because they have a good reward for their toil. For if they fall, one will lift up his fellow. But woe to him who is alone when he falls and has not another to lift him up!" (ESV)

What goes around, comes around. Lift up your friends, and they will do the same for you.

Removing Relationships

If you've decided to change your "friend structure" after reading this chapter, I just want to encourage you, sister. You can do this. You may have current "friends" that are not healthy relationships. They may drag you down, or expect too much from you without returning the love. Your friend might be cynical about her husband, and you may feel uncomfortable talking about yours. Maybe you become too involved with gossip or harmful speech when you are around each other. Whatever the negativity, consider if it is a friendship that God wants you to have.

Sometimes you need to break up with friends. You may decide to tell them that you need a break. If that's difficult for you, try to space your time with that person until it's nearly none. Give them anything that belongs to them and break ties that keep you bonded to an unhealthy relationship.

I know it seems easier said than done. Spend time in the Word and ask for wisdom to remove the toxic relationship.

Something that occurred to me as I wrote this chapter is the danger of man-and-woman relationships. If you are married or are going to become married, do not, under any circumstance, become great friends with a man. It will not be healthy for your relationship with your spouse, and you will be headed down a road of destruction.

Many men and women enter friendships with a naive notion that they will remain simply friends. Unfortunately, temptation always occurs suddenly. It always starts innocently, but inevitably becomes dangerous.

Even if the friendship doesn't become sexual, there are also temptations to fantasize about a life with the person. Comparing spouses, finances, complaints, among other things are common temptations when you allow yourself to be friends with a man who isn't your husband. This will cause you to become dissatisfied with your marriage on many accounts, and will also spur jealousy from your spouse.

If you have a friendship with a "couple," it's great to be friends with someone's husband. However it must be done very carefully. Any communication should include a spouse, and there should never be time spent alone together. Very clear boundaries must be adhered to. For instance, if a friend's husband texts you, simply respond with your own husband in the conversation. It doesn't have to be a giant drawn out conversation, just a simple boundary that will be set.

If you are currently in a deep friendship with a man, you need to run. Flee this friendship immediately and see your marriage flourish with blessing.

In Chapter 9: Homeschool 101, I discuss children having internships with close friends. This is done excellently with men and your sons. However, please do not send your daughters to be alone with a man either. Even if they are completely trusted, it will instill in your daughters good practice to keep their distance.

When you are setting up homeschool internships, or if you are working with a man for your business, try to include your husband in the details. With business, it becomes harder to distance yourself from men; however, by keeping things 100 percent professional, and not spending alone or personal time with a man, you'll still be working within boundaries. Make sure that your husband knows and agrees with whatever plan you choose regarding working with men.

Family Considerations

When you are deciding who to trust in your deep circle, you should consider family members. Some family members could be your parents or grandparents. You should consider your siblings and in-laws. Friends will come and go, but family is permanent. If you are blessed enough to have family in your deep relationship circle, you'll want nothing more. If possible, I genuinely recommend that you search this avenue first for your deep circle of friends.

Family can be such a great help with homeschooling, and for getting extra time to work your business. They love you and your children indefinitely, which becomes an incredible asset in your life.

Points to Ponder:

What areas can you cultivate trust with your husband?

Who is in your deep circle currently?

If you have more than four couples, who could you start to limit time with?

Do your friends share the same parental values as you? How? Who are they?

Do you have a spiritually supportive friendship?

Do you have family members that you could add to your circle?

Chapter Four

Spiritual Health

If you are going to make changes to have balance in your life, you will want to start with your spiritual health. You cannot become better at anything without spiritual reflection and growth. If you wish to have lasting effects from changes that you make, the changes must be grounded in Scripture. As I'm sure you have realized, I use Scripture to ground everything I do. This chapter is not different, but instead explains how you can ground yourself in Scripture too.

Have you ever read Proverbs 31? This is the chapter in the Bible that describes a perfect woman. The "Proverbs 31 woman" is:

- *Trustworthy*

- *Hardworking*

- *A researcher and learner*

- *Feeds her household healthy food*

- *Generous*

- *Excellent at time management*

- *Physically healthy and strong*

- *She is proactive*

- *Resourceful*

- *Vigilant*

- *Business owner*

- *Investor*

- *Teacher*

- *Active*

- *Manager*

- *Wife*

- *Gentle-spirited*

- *Wise*

- *Kind*

- *Honorable*

- *Adored by her children*

- *Praised by her husband*

- *Proud of her accomplishments*

- *Content*

- *Seeks the Lord in what she does*

Does this list of the "perfect woman" encourage or discourage you? Don't look at this list as an impossible feat to accomplish. Instead, see it as an attribute list of the woman you were created to become. Look for the areas of your life in which you demonstrate these characteristics. You have what it takes to become what God created you for.

I left space for your notes in the list above. Take a few minutes to look over every quality and write down how you currently achieve it or have made it in the past. If you can't think of anything, write down a way that you can achieve the quality.

Isn't that an encouraging exercise? If we focus through the lens of who God desires us to be, the more we naturally become that woman. Most things that God wants for women are reflected in this list. If your desires line up with God's, you'll be on your way to success. In your pursuit of balance, make sure that your goals can be connected to the Proverbs 31 list.

I'd love to walk you through the entire Proverbs 31 chapter, but this is not the book for that. Instead, let's dive into ways to apply biblical truths to achieve balance in your life while becoming the woman you are created to be.

When I began my mothering, homeschool, and business journey, I wanted to do it all successfully. How could I be a "Proverbs 31 Woman" and do it well?

The Bible has the answers we are looking for to help us become amazing women. Psalm 37:4 says, "Delight yourself in the Lord, and he will give you the desires of your heart" (ESV). If we are focused on pleasing the Lord with our desires, and if our ambitions align with God's direction for our lives, He will give us what it takes to achieve it.

Daily Reading

If you are going to learn how to grow spiritually, you must be reading the Bible daily. There is not any substitute for this. Joyce Meyer is a fantastic speaker, but she isn't the Bible. Your pastor might be excellent at teaching, but he isn't the Bible either. You must be reading the Bible, on your own, every day.

> 1 Chronicles 16:11 says, "Seek the Lord and his strength; seek his presence continually!" (ESV)

If you aren't currently reading the Bible each day, it might seem like a huge task to accomplish. But sister, it's worth it. After the habit has sunk in, you'll begin to crave and love when you sit with your cup of joe and your Bible. Nothing is better.

When you read Scripture daily, it allows God's Word to be molded onto your heart. When you are struggling in an area, or are looking for answers, you'll be surprised when you remember what was spoken in your daily Bible reading. Often, this is how God leads me in various directions in my life.

Daily reading the Bible is utterly necessary if you are going to become a woman who is capable of doing everything. If you are going to juggle 1,732 things at a time, there has to be a part of your day consistently grounded.

How do you go about starting? There are many Bible reading plans available online. These are great to motivate you to read from a checklist each day. Some of these reading plans are to read the Bible in one year. Some of the plans focus on specific topics. You can find a reading plan that will suit you perfectly—just do some Googling. There are even free Bible apps available that read aloud to you, and some have some excellent Bible studies.

Even though there are multiple reading plans and apps out there, I have found that they distract me from digging more in-depth with my learning. I prefer to read out of my physical Bible as opposed to an app. This is another way that I ground myself. Even just holding my Bible makes me feel grounded and aware that life is more important than myself. This is a trick that I have learned about myself. Try it. You might find that we have this in common.

At the moment, I am reading one chapter per day. I began in the gospel of John a couple months ago, and just continued on. This isn't a scheduled reading plan, but it works for me. I never feel behind if I accidentally sleep in, or if I have an early appointment. However, it gives me a marvelous reading plan that I can deeply explore each section.

In another chapter, I told you about my friend, Michelle, and how we read a chapter together every day. This has been incredibly helpful in holding me accountable for reading and digging deeper. Each day, we read a chapter individually. We each write notes about the section on a notebook, and then we text a picture of our notes to each other. It's been a fantastic way to learn on my own and learn from what she pulled out of it. It doesn't take any extra time to send her a text, and it gives me a more in-depth understanding.

How do I find time to read?

I know that this is going to be the number one question for most mamas. Having so many children has brought me through multiple life stages, and I wouldn't trade any of them for another. I'm going to share my experiences in stages, and maybe they will also work for you!

In the *pregnancy stage*, you're always exhausted. The last thing you want or can do is wake up with enough energy to read your Bible in the morning. I understand, but more importantly, so does God. He wants you to rest and care for your body. However, don't miss spending precious time with Him. During this stage, I found that mid-morning was the perfect time to read my Bible. After I woke up and ate breakfast, I usually had enough energy to keep my eyes open for a few minutes. If there are other little ones around, this is an excellent time for the children to have "sit time" while you study.

The *newborn and baby stage* is when you can't sleep a full night, either. You're utterly exhausted and spent on every level. Use this time wisely to spend bonding with your baby. I use my headphones to listen to Scripture during late night or early morning feedings during this stage. Don't try to balance nursing and holding a large Bible. Use this time to soak in Scripture being read to you. Enjoy that sweet time with your baby.

The *toddler and younger child stages* are terrific because you're finally able to sleep through the night! These are the stages where I train my little ones to stay in their room until 8:00 a.m. Many "light up" clocks will change color when it's time for them to get up. Use them as a resource to keep time balanced in your home. This allows you to wake up at 7:00 and get a cup of coffee and read alone.

For some reason, and I'm sure there is science to back it, God wants us to read in the morning. Here are some references that describe the mornings:

Psalm 5:3, "O LORD, in the morning you hear my voice; in the morning I prepare a sacrifice for you and watch" (ESV).

Psalm 90:14, "Satisfy us in the morning with your steadfast love, that we may rejoice and be glad all our days" (ESV).

Psalm 119:147, "I rise before dawn and cry for help; I hope in your words" (ESV).

Make a habit of reading at the same time each day, regardless of the stages you are at in your life. This will help you to make reading Scripture a priority.

Supported Scripture

Recently, my daughter Miranda had some questions about her future. She has a list of things that she wants to accomplish in her life and wondered if it was "okay" that she desired certain things. We looked at Scripture and saw that her desires are supported and encouraged.

"Mom, do you think it's silly that I desire to protect children as I do?" She asked me this question in such a sweet, humbling way, I could hardly respond without tearing up.

"Oh honey," I gasped. "It's not silly. In fact, protecting the innocent is in the Bible." I was so honored that she brought this question to me.

"But what if I never get to help them the way that I want to? I'm just so small, and I need to be strong to accomplish this." She said these words wearily, as if she had exhausted all of her thinking on the subject.

"Well, let's check with God," I said. We proceeded to look up Scripture regarding protecting the innocent and being a strong woman.

After searching scripture, we found these verses:

Psalm 82:3-4, "Give justice to the weak and the fatherless; maintain the right of the afflicted and the destitute. Rescue the weak and the needy; deliver them from the hand of the wicked" (ESV).

Ephesians 6:10, "Finally, be strong in the Lord and in the strength of his might" (NASB).

Proverbs 31:25, "Strength and dignity are her clothing. She laughs at the time to come" (NHEB).

After reading these Scriptures together, I said, "See honey? Everything you desire to do is supported by Scripture. God will even give you the strength to do it! God desires you to do these things. He gave you an extra dose of desire in this particular area. Own it."

In this real example of my life, do you see how Scripture can and should be used? If you have a desire, check with Scripture to keep your goals in line with God's.

> "Do not be anxious about anything, but in everything by prayer and supplication with thanksgiving let your requests be made known to God. And the peace of God, which surpasses all understanding, will guard your hearts and minds in Christ Jesus" (Philippians 4:6-7, ESV).

When you ask God about your desires and look for Scripture to answer your questions, you will gain direction and peace.

Context Warning

I just want to quickly mention context. When you begin to use Scripture to define your life, please use the Bible in context. Frequently, people will see a plaque or picture that says a Bible verse that they like, and then use it to apply to their situation. Unfortunately, the Bible doesn't work this way. You must read Scripture thoroughly so that you know what it is referencing.

An example of the importance of context is Jeremiah 29:11.

We've all seen a framed verse that says, "I know the plans I have for you. Plans to prosper you and plans to give you hope and a future." This Scripture is powerful on 800 levels. However, it doesn't mean that you will become filthy rich, and whatever you put your hand to is going to prosper. Many people misuse this Bible verse every day.

When you ask God about your desires and look for Scripture to answer your questions, you will gain direction and peace.

Jeremiah 29:11 is quite impressive in context: God is talking to Israel while they are heading into exile. God is telling the Israelites that He won't stay angry at them forever. He was sending a savior (Jesus) who would come to be their hope of salvation.

From this, we learn that God doesn't stay angry with us. He loves us, even when we mess up. He thinks about us and has plans for our future! This says that He gives us Jesus to be our hope and future. Nothing can separate us from His love.

I don't know about you, but I think this verse's real meaning is much more powerful than the "filthy rich" version.

Do you see how important it is to know Scripture as a whole, instead of small tidbits that you hear or read on Facebook? Spend time reading and studying. I promise you, sister, this will be the best decision you've ever made.

Reflection & Focus

Every morning, I wake up early, and I snuggle into the La-Z Boy with my feet up. I sip my coffee slowly. I stare at my Bible, and before I even pick it up, I ask God to teach me something. I pick up my Bible and flip to the section that I left off the day before. I have two notebooks with me. One is my "Prayer Journal," and the other is just my regular journal. I turn my regular journal to a new page and use it as my "Thinking" page. This is how I begin each morning. It's funny because even as I write this description for you, I long for coffee and a pen in my hand. Tomorrow can't come soon enough.

When I sit down to read, I purposefully leave my phone in another room. I am easily distracted by it. If there is something that I want to look up, I just make a note of it. Before I began the habit of leaving my phone in the other room, I would sometimes waste my entire alone time by "looking up" things. Don't fall into the same trap. Leave your phone plugged in somewhere else.

As I read my daily chapter, I reflect on what I'm reading. I make notes in my prayer journal. I'll also use my footnotes in the Bible to find correlating scripture and read those sometimes. It's a fantastic learning hour.

When I'm done reading, I grab my thinking page. I learned about a thinking page from the book *How Successful People Think* by John Maxwell.

The "thinking page" is a reflection and thought process spot for planning your day or business ideas. Anything that you need to think about, do it now. If you allow yourself time to think, plan, and develop new ideas, nothing can hold you back from becoming better at life. Take notes while you think and use them throughout your day as you are in school, parenting, or doing business.

Whether you are writing in your prayer journal or your thinking page, just make sure to write. Don't let the pen sit down. The point of writing is to keep you focused on what you are doing. If you are reading Scripture, then write down what you're learning, even if it's every sentence. If you are thinking about business ideas, write them out as you think about them. You might never use the ideas, but it will keep your mind focused.

Main Focus

In 1 Corinthians 3, Paul talks about how God gives each person an individual task. We were not all created to do the same thing in this life. Each of us has gifts and talents that God gives us. We need to make sure that as we use these gifts and move forward in our tasks, our motives are based on Jesus' desires. He wants our focus to be on Him alone. Everything else is meaningless.

How can your business or homeschooling lessons be based on Him? I think it depends on your goals. If your goal is to be filthy rich and drive an expensive car, that's a lame goal.

If your desire is to support your family while raising your children, that's a godly goal. The Bible talks about how important it is to provide for your family. It also talks about how vital raising children is. Having goals that are in line with God's Word is what He desires for us.

Don't forget to check the Proverbs 31 attributes list. Make sure that your goals fall into one of those categories.

Points to Ponder:

Look at the Proverbs 31 attributes list again. What is your greatest desire?

Why are you reading this book?

Do you feel capable of accomplishing everything that you desire?

Are your desires supported by Scripture?

What time of day will you habitually read your Bible?

Have you ever seen Scripture taken out of context?

What is your main focus?

Chapter Five

Physical Health

Did you know that physical health affects proficiency? Anything that affects your body also affects your mind. If you want to achieve stress-free balance in your life, you need to prioritize physical health.

The Bible talks extensively about caring for the body. God makes it abundantly clear that He cares about our physical health. First Corinthians 6 tells us that God made our bodies to be used for His purposes. It also says that the Holy Spirit lives in our mortal bodies, paid a high price for our bodies, and is honored when we care for our bodies.

Don't forget, mama: your children are watching how you care for yourself. Whatever you choose, they will follow. If you wish to be health-conscious, they will too. If you care for your body, they will care for theirs as well. If they see you confidently looking in the mirror, they will too. You must parent them and teach them how to properly care for their physical health. I know this task might seem daunting, but fear not! We have a "guidebook" for success in health. If God is concerned about our physical health, we should look in Scripture at how He tells us to care for ourselves.

Food

In our health-conscious society, many people are finally aware that health begins in the kitchen. You can be a gymnast, professional athlete, or a marathon runner. Still, nothing will keep you healthier than the food you nourish your body with.

The Bible talks a great deal about nourishing foods for your body.

Genesis 1:29, "And God said, 'Behold, I have given you every plant yielding seed that is on the face of all the earth, and every tree with seed in its fruit. You shall have them for food'" (ESV).

Genesis 9:3, "Every moving thing that lives shall be food for you. And as I gave you the green plants, I give you everything" (ESV).

Psalm 104:15b, "…bread to strengthen man's heart" (ESV).

1 Corinthians 9:27, "But I discipline my body and keep it under control, lest after preaching to others I myself should be disqualified" (ESV).

There are many schools of thought on diet and which direction is the best for optimum health. It can be frustrating to read about veganism, ketogenic, low-fat, low-carb, whole foods, or any number of diet plans. Do yourself a favor and save your brain space. These eating plans make sense in part, but I have tried several diet plans and wrecked my metabolism. Without adequate calories and balanced macronutrients, you cannot be in optimum health.

We all have different needs, and one diet can't possibly work for everyone.

Every body type and shape is different. We all have different needs, and one diet can't possibly work for everyone. However, there is a lifestyle that I have found that has rescued millions of women. It's called *Trim*

Healthy Mama (THM). If I could recommend a book more than any other book (other than the Bible, of course), I would always put *Trim Healthy Mama* first. It has changed my life entirely.

The homeschooling sisters that wrote THM use a biblical approach to eating sustainably. I'm thankful that I will never worry about being overweight again, and I can eat delicious foods that I love. Please do yourself a favor and read their book for yourself. You'll never go back to anything else. Even if you can't afford to purchase the book yourself, try to get it from your local library. Trust me, sister, this needs to be in your arsenal.

Since I've been a "Trim Healthy Mama" for a few years, my food view has changed. Food used to be an obsession and a stumbling block for me. I would live to eat, live to drink wine, and I gained plenty of pounds from it. I enjoyed "health food," but too much of it. This caused me to have imbalanced hormones and a large body shape.

Now, I enjoy food and eat decadent desserts that I never thought were allowed. I find myself craving healthy salads and buttered vegetables. I can listen to my body and nourish it with food instead of feeling bound to unhealthy cravings. I'm thirty-five years old and in the best shape of my life. When you can manage your relationship with food, you'll be a massive step toward a life of balance.

Eating healthy is the first step to gaining optimum health. Choose to nourish your body with healthy foods. It's important to realize that there is a bit of self-control required when you break food addictions. The Bible tells us that we can discipline our bodies and keep them under restraint.

Many people have differing opinions on what constitutes "healthy." Going by what the Bible says, combined with modern science, I will leave a sample list here of some of my favorite healthy food choices.

Veggies. Veggies. Veggies (unlimited quantities).

- Veggies include all types of green vegetables
- Carrots, squash, radishes, tomatoes, etc.

- Any and all frozen vegetables
- A small number of sweet potatoes
- Avoid corn and regular potatoes

Fleshy fruits (pears, peaches, apples, nectarines, etc.)

Naturally sugar-free sweeteners like stevia, monk fruit, or erythritol

High-protein dairy

Fat-free Greek yogurt

Low-fat cottage cheese

Hard cheeses

One-third less fat cream cheese

Heavy cream

Kefir

Cocoa powder or high-percent chocolate

Meats and eggs of all kinds

Low glycemic grains

- Oatmeal
- Soaked or sprouted wheat
- Sourdough bread
- No pasta or white bread
- Millet

Brown rice, not white

Barley

Nuts and natural nut butter (all types)

Fats

- Coconut oil

- Olive oil

- Ghee

- Butter

- Animal fats

Absolutely no processed or packaged food

Absolutely no added sugar

Some can tolerate small amounts of honey, but this can cause weight gain for many mamas, so I avoid it altogether.

> In fact, the Bible discusses honey a little as well in Proverbs 25:27. It says, "It is not good to eat much honey, nor is it glorious to seek one's own glory" (ESV).

I think that it's interesting that honey is compared with selfish ambition in this verse. When we eat sugary treats and can't control ourselves, it's often that inner selfish ambition at work inside of us…some food for thought.

If you read the *Trim Healthy Mama* book, the healthy food list is much more expanded than this list. However, I wanted to give you a base to start from while we discuss a healthy lifestyle.

Mealtimes and Portion Sizes

How often you eat makes a difference in your body. If you have weight to lose or if you are trying to balance your hormones, you want to assure your body that you aren't starving. When your body gets a "starving" signal, it holds onto each pound and doesn't balance hormones properly.

Instead of going on extreme calorie restrictions or intermittent fasting, consider eating every three hours. I know that this sounds opposite of the weight loss gurus. Doing this will allow your body to recognize that it's getting adequate nutrition.

Personally, my family eats at the same times each day. I prefer to do this because it helps in the structure of my home. By having set meal times, everyone knows what time to show up in the kitchen.

We eat at 8–9 a.m., 12 p.m., 3 p.m., and 6 p.m. Our family rarely does any snacking after dinner unless it's a piece of chocolate immediately after dinner. We also do not snack in between meals. This allows our bodies to properly process the food that we have ingested.

By eating every three hours, you'll rarely feel hungry in between meals, so the tendency to overeat is less of an issue. Overeating is actually discussed in Scripture as well.

Proverbs 23:2, "And put a knife to your throat if you are given to appetite" (ESV).

Proverbs 23:21, "For the drunkard and the glutton will come to poverty, and slumber will clothe them with rags" (ESV).

How can you eat healthily and eat proper portion sizes without starving all the time? It's about learning balance. When you fill your plate, put on enough food that will last you for three hours. You'll get the hang of this quickly. Aim for 15–20 grams of protein, and add a plethora of vegetables. You might decide to add some healthy carbs or some healthy fats with your meal. If you fill up on the vegetables, followed by protein, you will feel satisfied.

I personally like to pile high with greens. I began doing this because I genuinely enjoy eating. I wanted the hand-to-mouth action more than I was getting with smaller portion sizes. By eating my salad out of a mixing bowl (this is not a joke!), I get more than enough hand-to-mouth action. Sometimes I feel tired of eating when I'm done. Try "tricks" like this to give you satisfaction with your food and become accustomed to eating regularly.

Meal Planning

When you get started down the "healthy food" journey, you might feel overwhelmed by the amount of food that needs to be homemade. You might also think that you don't have brain space to think very far ahead for meals.

This is where I can teach you a thing or two about meal planning. Push up your sleeves, sister, grab a notebook, and let's plan out some healthy meals for your family.

Meal planning saves me an incredible amount of time each week. It also saves money on my grocery bill. You would think that after having children for sixteen years, I'd have a pretty good idea of what to cook for dinner each night. Well...I don't. Just like you, my day becomes busy very quickly. I plan ahead as much as I can. Still, I sometimes forget to get frozen items out to thaw or possibly forget to purchase something at the grocery store. Even with meal planning, there will be days that you get caught off guard, but not often. I'll share my secret system with you, so you can be successful at this.

Here's a step-by-step tutorial to write an excellent meal list.

> *Begin your list by writing the day of the week and the date that you are beginning.*

When you begin a meal plan, you want to write down dates and days of the week. I know this is silly, but I always write the dates. I keep my previous meal plans to look back on for fresh ideas.

> *Write (B)reakfast, (L)unch, (D)inner underneath each day.*

Make every second count when you are balancing your life.

I used to only write out dinner plans on my meal list. When I began homeschooling, I realized that I needed to have an all-day plan. My older children often help with the meals, and they can quickly look at my list. It also helps me avoid standing in front of the fridge while trying to decide what's for breakfast and lunch—make every second count when you are balancing your life.

> *If you have anything on the calendar that will affect meal times being*

93

early or late, write them next to the date.

You'll love this tip. By writing your calendared items on your meal plan, you can write in "on the go" meals or dinners for which you need quick clean-up. This is also an excellent way for you to see what days you can let the children cook with you. Sometimes I even check the weather to see what days I want to grill outside.

Look through your fridge, freezer, and pantry to plan meals with items that you already have.

You'll be surprised to find a head of lettuce sitting in your crisper, or an extra bag of mozzarella cheese. You might even find some spare ribs in the freezer and have a BBQ! Whatever you do, do not go to the grocery store without knowing what you already have. This will help you save money, and rotate the food in your stash so that nothing gets wasted.

Keep a second notebook next to you to write a grocery list for items that you don't have.

When I write my grocery list throughout the week, it's very minimal until I have a meal plan. This is when all the good stuff gets added. I don't really use a paper list for this. Instead, I use a grocery pick-up app on my phone.

Try to plan the meal around a protein source. I like to alternate my protein sources.

Protein is the building block of health. You absolutely need it for each meal. Typically I will save meat for dinners. Although sometimes I'll have leftover meat for lunch. I will often pack my husband lunches from the previous night's dinner, so I don't worry about him with our lunch plans. He needs more protein than my children and I require. The children and I also do a lot of soups during the week. It's a cheap and easy meal usually loaded with beans or lentils that give us high protein and fiber.

Start writing your plan.

This is the fun part. Write in all the yummy foods that you can think of! I like to look through my cookbooks for inspiration too. Also, think about the weather. If it's cold outside, try to plan at least two soups per week. If it's mid-July, think about cold salads and grilling.

Add in the "only you" items.

This is very important. My children know that I have different needs than they do, so they are not surprised when I eat something different at breakfast or lunch. I always eat the same meal for dinner with my family—although I might go light on the cheese. My children can eat grilled cheese sandwiches without a problem, but my waistline explodes if I do. So when I write in "grilled cheese," I will add in my food next to it in parenthesis, such as (salmon salad).

Need an example? Here is a four-day example meal list that I made for you. I will typically plan two weeks at once to save time. Sunday is a perfect day to write a meal plan. A two-week list will take me about 30–60 minutes to write. Once it's written, you don't have to think about food until you write the next meal plan. I tape my meal list to the fridge for easy viewing. This is also helpful for the family to help with meal prepping if I'm unavailable.

Monday 7/1 (lunch playdate with Sam)

B) Eggs and toast (Egg whites/Toast)

L) Pack turkey sandwiches & pickles

D) Sourdough pizza with bacon/pineapple

Tuesday 7/2

B) Oatmeal with Yogurt & Blueberries

L) Microwave cheese tortillas (Salmon Salad)

D) Grilled burgers/potatoes/green beans (Sub radishes for potatoes)

Wednesday 7/3 (Worship team practice 6 p.m.)

B) Toast with cottage cheese & peanut butter (skip PB, sub egg whites)

L) Lentil soup

D) Crockpot BBQ pork sandwiches & side salad

Thursday 7/4 (Movie night.* Eat light.)

B) Yogurt parfait/blueberries/raspberries/oatmeal

L) Egg salad sandwiches and carrot sticks

D) Small chicken salad.

*make popcorn for movie

Enjoying Food with Others

Food is meant to be enjoyed. The Bible makes a big deal about enjoying food with others. In Scripture, you see multiple examples of meaningful conversations that took place at mealtimes. Please use these examples to learn to sit down at mealtime with as many people as you can. If you have multiple children, try to sit together to eat and talk during the day. If your husband is home, sit down and enjoy him while you eat.

Are family or friends coming to visit? Make meal time a delight, and invite them to stay. Always prepare too much food. You never know who you may be able to invite to sit at your table.

When you eat, you actually release endorphins in your brain. These puppies are the "feel-good" hormones. When you release endorphins while spending time with other people, there are incredible bonds that can develop.

The Proverbs 31 woman "provides food for her household and a portion for her maidservants." Coming from Eastern culture (people in the Middle East take meal time very seriously), I bet she provided the food and ate it with her household. People like a good cook, but love someone who spends time with them. Enjoy sitting down and eating with others.

Wine and Sugar

Wine is one of those topics that many Christians disagree on. Some people believe that a small amount is okay. Some believe that all alcohol is from the devil. Still, other people believe that wine is healthy and to be enjoyed regularly. Our society gives wine a "classy" view. Have you seen all the wine jokes on Pinterest recently? It doesn't take very long to see that our culture associates wine drinking as a classy way to unwind each day. Regardless of your views on alcohol, I want to discuss a couple things about addictions in general.

Sugar, alcohol, and caffeine all have addictive qualities that can throw your body out of balance and cause your brain to misfire. Hangovers from too much alcohol can hinder your concentration, but are you aware that your focus is also affected by sugar? Many homeschool acquaintances have told me that sugar and food dye removal have significantly helped ADD and ADHD symptoms in their children. A child that my family knows with autism is also greatly affected by sugar. His episodes are less intense when sugar is avoided. If the avoidance of sugar so clearly helps those with mental disorders, it is a safe assumption that it affects people who do not have mental disorders. Because I have seen how sugar affects the body, I prefer to completely avoid it in my home. This includes most natural sugars like honey and maple syrup as well.

I personally enjoy a glass of wine at any time. However, I am extra cautious about controlling my wine intake instead of it controlling me. This means that I must distance myself from it at most times, even if I want to enjoy a glass. One glass tonight can easily turn to two glasses tomorrow for me. If you struggle with over-consuming wine, you are not alone, sister. I feel you.

I have also noticed having a glass or two of wine in the evening will create a foggy brain the next day and the day after that. Literally, two days of intense focus and peace can be squandered in one night of have a relaxing sip for some. That seems to defeat the purpose of relaxing.

There are a lot of opinions of people who drink wine. However, for some reason, no one ever admits that it's a problem.

Drinking wine is drinking alcohol. It's the same thing. You can be addicted to it.

If you feel like you should hide your drinking, you are probably drinking too often.

Drinking wine can still be a problem, even if you think it's "trendy" or socially acceptable.

If you are thinking about wine periodically during the day, you probably should give yourself a break.

I have a beautiful friend named Marie, who I get to catch up with every few months. I learn many things from her, including the ability to self-reflect. During many conversations, she has told me about her frustration of drinking wine. She enjoys wine, and has it almost daily, yet she has noticed that she is increasingly irritable with her family. Marie believes that wine is the culprit of her frustrations. Unfortunately, she has struggled with these feelings for years.

To someone who doesn't drink, it's easy to say, "Stop drinking to fix the problem!" However, it's easier said than done. When a person develops a habit that is fueled by addiction, it can be a vicious cycle to break. Even people with the best intentions, like Marie, can get stuck in a place of self-hatred, but lacks the ability to stop.

When we spend all day at home with our children and working on business, it becomes easy to pour a wine glass in the afternoon or evening. We don't have anyone at home keeping us accountable. If your husband drinks, he will also have a glass with you, which leads to another and another.

Drinking wine can seriously hinder your progress in your family, budget, and business growth. Since I have struggled in this area, I want to give you a few tips that have helped me enjoy wine in limited amounts, and control my desire.

I give you these ideas because if you are spending time lamenting about drinking, I want to show you a way out.

Take supplements for your liver.

We all know that the liver is the detoxifier of the body. Alcohol can significantly increase the workload of the liver. By supporting the liver, I personally have less alcohol cravings. When I take dandelion root, milk thistle, and kudzu for liver support, I have zero alcohol cravings. I never even think about it. I think the herbs work by helping to detoxify the liver from all of the alcohol-related toxins. By doing this, our body can process new areas of the body and make you feel fantastic. When you feel terrific, you don't desire to add pollutants into your body.

Find something to do in the afternoons.

I realized that my favorite time to drink wine is about 4:00 p.m. Because of this, I try to go somewhere. I enjoy going to the library or walking in the park with the children. These are great ways to get out of the house and avoid drinking hour. You have to do this intentionally. It takes effort and practice, but you'll be successful at it if you make plans ahead of time.

Don't buy it.

I know this sounds obvious, but if you don't have the wine in your house, you're less likely to have an intense craving terrible enough to buy some.

Read a book.

I truly enjoy reading a novel or a book in the evenings. If I drink wine, I am basically giving up my reading time because I can't focus. If I am reading a good novel, the last thing that I want to do is have a glass of wine. I just want to read.

Strength and Exercise

Have you ever had an injury that makes you unable to use your body correctly? When this happens, it's as if everything else disappears. You can't be content unless you get the physical ability back. If you lost the ability to walk, it would feel debilitating.

Walking would become the only thing you would think of.

Aaron, my husband, was born with a short femur. Because of this, his left leg was always about six inches shorter than his right. Eventually, he had his foot amputated at 13 years old to wear his prosthetic leg properly. Because of swelling during post-surgery, he could not wear his prosthetic leg for several weeks, and the inability to move was difficult for him to bear.

Thankfully, Aaron's parents were always supportive and required him to keep up with everyone else. He never felt different with his missing foot because he was never treated differently than others. During the healing period, however, they encouraged him to rest. This was difficult for Aaron, and walking became the only thing on his mind.

As soon as he was healed enough to be upright with his new prosthetic, he was walking, jumping, and running. There wasn't anything holding him back. He's had some frustrating events and random pains throughout the years, but there isn't anything that can keep him from moving. I know that he will be this way until he leaves this earth.

What I learn from Aaron's story is that my excuses to stay sitting are really lame. God created my body to move, and to move well. If Aaron can run two miles, then so can you and I! You might laugh at the idea of running, but it's a gift when you can accomplish it.

Many people in this world have situations that literally keep them from moving how their bodies were designed. In a way, it almost feels like honoring them when we use our bodies. When you exercise, and you're uncomfortable, don't give up. Instead, be thankful that you've been given the physical capabilities to do it.

Hitting personal goals is one of my favorite things. By incorporating some exercise in your life, adding in personal goals, and achieving them, you begin to develop great satisfaction in yourself. You start to believe in yourself as well.

To be successful in any homeschool or business adventure, you must believe in yourself. If you can reach goals in exercise, you will feel confident that you can reach your goals in business too.

Proverbs 31:17, "She girds herself with strength and strengthens her" (NKJV).

Sometimes moving your body is as simple as a brisk walk. Sometimes it's doing some push-ups or running on the treadmill. Whatever your level of exercise is, take it one step further. You were created to move. Strengthen your body, mama.

When you are considering exercise in your life, go with a balanced approach. There is not a reason to go to the gym and pour sweat each day when you are trying to balance many areas of your life. In fact, if you are just beginning an exercise routine, ease into it. Otherwise you might become frustrated by unattainable goals.

Start by doing a twenty-minute YouTube video, or go for a half-mile jog. Another idea is to get your kids moving as a class in homeschool. I'll include some great kid's exercise YouTube channels in the connections chapter. Working out with your kids is fun, and you won't need to worry about finding extra time in your day to be alone.

Sleep

Stressed people don't usually sleep well. When they awaken, since they haven't had adequate rest, their brains and bodies have not been rejuvenated. This causes the effect of high cortisol in the body. High cortisol causes more stress, and the cycle gets worse. As you sleep less, your body also stops digesting efficiently. Poor digestion causes weight gain, diseases, and sickness.

Repeat after me, "I will sleep and not be anxious!" If Jesus is your King, you are not a woman who is bound by anxious thoughts. You are a woman who trusts that God is bringing you through a chapter in your life that you can manage with His help. After all, without Him, you are nothing. Everything you are doing is in HIS hands.

Psalm 127:2, "It is in vain that you rise up early and go late to rest, eating the bread of anxious toil; for he gives to his beloved sleep" (ESV).

Proverbs 3:24, "If you lie down, you will not be afraid; when you lie down, your sleep will be sweet" (NIV).

Psalm 4:8, "In peace, I will both lie down and sleep; for you alone, O Lord, make me dwell in safety" (ESV).

Stress and anxiety can definitely be a genuine factor in your life that causes sleeplessness. If stress or anxiety is keeping you awake at night, I strongly suggest having downtime before bed. Try to give yourself at least an hour before bed to keep screens away from your eyes. This allows your brain to slow down. In fact, even if you stay up late, simply to give yourself an hour, you'll find that sleep may be sweeter.

Also consider reading a novel. I know that sounds silly or cliché, but if you are reading a novel at bedtime, you might find that your brain can shut off the outside noise that is keeping you awake.

Many people who are stressed struggle with fear. They fear that they will miss a deadline. Business owners fear that they are forgetting an important detail. Parents have doubts that they are making the right decision. Homeschoolers fear they aren't teaching their children well enough.

Regardless of the reasons behind the fears, we need to let them go. God doesn't want us to miss out on precious sleep because of worries. Did He bring you this far in your life? Do you have new opportunities that are in line with the Word? If so, then sister, you need to lay those fears down and get some sleep.

Another cause of sleeplessness when you are balancing many projects at once is lack of nutrition. You must nourish your body with healthy food if you are going to get precious sleep. Just because you are busy, it is no excuse for eating improperly. If you aren't hungry, it's not a valid reason to skip meals either. Your body needs nutrition, regardless if you are hungry at the moment or not. Use the clock to determine your meal times...not your feelings.

When my body was in the slow healing process after yo-yo dieting, I went through a time when I couldn't sleep through the night. It was incredibly frustrating. However, once my diet became regular and balanced with biblical concepts, I began to sleep better. I also discovered that having some gentle carbs at dinner time increases my deep sleep during the night. Another discovery is if I feel hungry before bed, I will make a cup of tea with a scoop of collagen n it for protein. This also helps me to fall into deep sleep quicker than if I stayed hungry.

Points to Ponder:

What is your current relationship with food?

What areas can you eat healthier?

What meals can you include in a meal list?

Who was the last person that you enjoyed food with?

What is a way that you can strengthen yourself physically?

When can you schedule sleep time for yourself?

What are ways that you can become positive in your thinking?

Is there anything that you should discuss with a doctor?

Is wine addiction a problem in your life? How can you overcome it?

Chapter Six

Mental & Emotional Health

Since you are becoming a balanced mama, having a healthy brain is a step that you must take. By now, we've discussed sleeping, eating, praying, healthy relationships, and your desires. As I'm sure you are aware, having an imbalance in any of these areas can cause stress. Stress affects your mental health. Let's look at some important things regarding your mind and how we can keep it healthy.

Body and Mind

Your mind is connected to your body. I'm sure that you've heard people say things like, "Imagine yourself thin if you want to be thin." They aren't joking. The power of the mind is incredible. When we can harness the mind's power, our body's health will benefit significantly from it. This is even biblically supported!

3 John 1:2, "Beloved, I pray that all may go well with you and that you may be in good health, as it goes well with your soul" (ESV).

Proverbs 17:22, "A joyful heart is good medicine, but a crushed spirit dries up the bones" (ESV).

Proverbs 14:30, "A tranquil heart gives life to the flesh, but envy makes the bones rot" (ESV).

Do you see how important it is to think positively? Sometimes it's hard to be positive in unfavorable scenarios. When I told you in a previous chapter about my husband's love of the fan, it was not an easy task to change my thinking. However, it can be done. When you tell yourself something, your brain will eventually believe it.

Many women have made themselves thin by merely repeating to themselves, "I love healthy food." Smokers have overcome their addictions by saying, "No, thanks. I don't smoke." Broken marriages have been revived by saying, "I'm sorry." Regardless of the words that you speak, you must realize that they will affect your brain. All words affect your brain.

I have a soup that I love to make. I call it "tornado soup." It's really just a puréed squash soup, but I had a tactical plan when I named it. You see, my family thinks that squash is boring. When I used to make squash soup, I would get looks that showed disappointment. One stormy day, during a wicked rainstorm, I was cooking up some squash soup. As I pureed it into a liquid, I thought it looked similar to a tornado. Considering that it was storming, I decided to make a big deal about this fun "new tornado soup" recipe. My family loved it! In fact, for months, I would get requests for tornado soup for supper.

Just by saying an interesting name, my family decided that they loved tornado soup. As hilarious as this sounds, it's because the brain is affected by what we say. I created an interesting name, which led to my family to become interested in the soup. It was the same recipe of soup that I made before...yet they all deemed it amazing.

How can you use these tactics to balance your life? Well, my dear sister, grab your notebook. Let's turn your stresses and negative thoughts into positive ones. This will give you peace and balance in any area of your life.

On a notebook page, I want you to write these questions. Give each item enough space to write some answers.

- What things frustrate me in my homeschool?

- What is hard for me to accomplish in homeschool?

- What things frustrate me in my business?

- What is holding me back in my business?

- What monotonous job do I loathe doing?

Decide what things you have negative thoughts about. Go ahead and write them down. When you see how much you may be negative about, it might surprise you.

Once you have determined your negative thoughts, begin to think of ways to change their position in your mind. Write these positive thoughts in your notebook.

"I don't have enough individual teaching time with each child."

By spinning this frustration into a positive, I decided to rephrase, "I'm thankful that I have this many kids to teach. They learn so much more from each other."

When you begin this exercise, it feels forced. It's okay. Do it anyway. You will notice the next time you have a negative feeling, you can quickly pull out your positive words. Say them out loud. Make your brain believe the positive.

Make your brain believe the positive.

Mental Disorders

Mental disorders can be caused by a plethora of things. I won't pretend to know it all. However, I have seen how loss and grief are incredibly hard to bear. If you've never experienced grief in this way, there isn't anything to describe it, other than if you were to understand agonizing physical pain. People who suffer loss will often have a sense of doom themselves. Grieving almost always causes a form of depression, anxiety, or mental disorder. Sometimes grief causes physical symptoms of illnesses because your brain and body cannot take the stress induced from your pain. Some people who commit suicide from grief do so because they genuinely think they can't take any more pain.

Although I never attempted or contemplated suicide, I was hurting significantly and wished that I would die. I would often cry out to God, "Please just take me to be with you now. I can't be here one more day."

Grief takes its time, and I knew it. But I hated that my brain and body wouldn't respond to usual cues. I had extreme anxiety and depression, which kept me from doing anything that I loved. I have no memory of two years of my life. My brain just couldn't hold onto anything. I call that hurting time my "lost years."

I still was in this type of grieving time in 2016 when I discovered that I was pregnant with my youngest, Joy. I remember vividly, crying out to God, "What are you thinking?! How can I take care of a baby if I can't even care for myself?"

During one of these agonizing prayers, I remembered the verse,

> "weeping may stay for the night, but rejoicing comes in the morning" (Psalm 30:5, NIV).

God was going to give me joy. In the midst of all of my grief and sorrow, God would bring joy into my life. He was using a sweet, innocent baby to bring me back to life.

I had Joy's name chosen when I was only twelve weeks pregnant. I knew that she was God's merciful gift to bring my heart and mind back to life.

When Joy was born, she was everything that we could hope for. However, I still struggled with severe depression and anxiety. I tried multiple herbs and supplements, but nothing would cut the "raw" feeling and cloudy thinking.

Against my natural and holistic background, I eventually went to a conventional doctor who put me on antidepressants. If I could change the past, I wouldn't have waited as long as I did. Within a month, I began to feel more like myself. I started smiling again. I could listen to music without an anxiety attack. I was able to enjoy each precious moment with Joy, and I remembered them! Things began to get better quickly.

From what I understand, people who suffer stress trauma can have altered brain function for the rest of their lives. The added stress of depression and anxiety will compound the issue to be worse. Without treatment, these conditions will keep the person in mental instability permanently.

It's been a couple years since I began this medication. I've had a couple of adjustments, but I'm thankful each day for the "gentleness" that the medication allows me to have. If I have to stay on it permanently, I will never complain. Now I can be the mother that I desire, the wife that I was made to be, and be stress free. I will live in joy and feel peace.

The point of sharing my story with you is to show you that mental conditions are genuine. They can happen to anyone at any time. Sometimes mental ailments start slowly and etch away at your joy. However, in many cases, it comes on quickly. A lifetime of stress that finally reaches its max can profoundly change your brain.

God is the ultimate healer of our bodies. He gives us wisdom and grace in times that we are struggling. If you have depression or anxiety, do not merely say, "God will give me peace. I don't need the doctor." Mental disorders are not the kind of stress that the Bible refers to in Philippians 4:6. This was a struggle of mine for a long time, and I don't want you to face the same lie that I did.

God is the ultimate healer of our bodies.

You've never heard someone say, "My leg is cut off and gushing blood, but God will heal me. I'm not going to the doctor." That's ridiculous. We have hospitals and medication for a reason. They are for sick people. God gives unique wisdom and capabilities to doctors for our good.

Your brain and mind are also part of your physical body. Sometimes we can become injured or sick. Please see a doctor if you have difficulty in this area.

We need to think about our health as our physical, spiritual, and mental health combined. God made our bodies in His image (Genesis 1:27), so we should expect that we would be wonderfully complex. It's no wonder that these aspects of our health tie together so closely. You have been made with a purpose. Your relationship to food, your body, God, and your thoughts are all part of his masterful plan.

As you consider how to be a successful homeschooler, or how to take your business to the next level, remember that if one part of you suffers, many parts will suffer. Be proactive in caring for your health, and you will be proactive in being successful in your life.

Points to Ponder:

What are areas in your life that you are naturally positive about?

Why are you positive about them?

What are some things that you struggle with or feel negative about?

What Scripture verses apply to these things?

Do you or someone you know struggle with mental disorders?

How can you be a blessing to yourself or others in this area?

Chapter Seven

Working at Home

Before exploring *how* to work at home, I want to take a few minutes to ponder why you should work at home. There are multiple schools of thought on this subject, and I don't claim to have all the answers. I'm simply going to walk you through my experiences and thought process in the hopes that you can identify with at least some of the concepts.

Doing What You Love

What is something that you love to do? What are you inherently good at? Sometimes if you are asked for advice on a subject, it's because you show talent in a certain area. Pay attention to areas in your life that you excel in.

Whatever that "something" is, you can help others and make money doing it. You have been given unique abilities that are natural for you.

Do you have a lot of interest in a particular subject? Or do you have strong skills in an area of your life? These are the starting points of business for yourself. God blesses us with natural abilities that can generate income. If you don't have a business idea yet, explore your interests and imagine how you can use them as an enjoyable job. If you already have a business started, consider how you can gear it more toward your interests, gifts, and talents.

Our current family business started this way. When we began our web design business, we had skills, and others needed our help. My husband had been building websites and doing design work for years. He was known in the community for his sharp business sense, graphic design, and web-building capabilities. People would call frequently to ask for business advice or help building their websites. Of course, we would help them. After all, it was the loving thing to do. We were honored that we were trusted by others, and we chose to help them any way that we could.

Although we liked the idea of building our own business, we weren't in a hurry to do so because we were fully content with my husband's 9–5 web design job. One day, we had a conversation that would change our life forever.

It started with a simple favor for our mechanic. Over the years, we have developed a friendship with the owners. They asked us to help them with their web presence, so we built them a website and helped build their business clientele.

> One day, I was picking up my van from their shop. When I walked into the shop to get my keys, Linda (the owner) said brightly, "I'd like to have a stack of business cards of yours to hand out to our business group. They're meeting this week, and I want to tell everyone about what a great job you did on our website."

> "Oh!" I exclaimed. I cleared my throat, and replied calmly, "We don't have business cards. We do this for people when they need us, but we haven't made this our full-time business. I'm not even sure we'd get enough clients to support us."

> Linda stared at me blankly for a couple seconds. "Elizabeth," She spoke in a motherly tone. "There isn't anyone in town that we would rather do business with. You do an amazing job, and we want to refer you out. You will get more than enough clients to support your family. This community sticks together. Go tell your husband to make business cards today."

> After that conversation, we started to think more seriously about our web business. Linda gave us courage and vision we didn't realize we needed. We eventually began Singler Design, and we love every second of what we do.

On top of loving our job, we have also discovered how much of a blessing it is for my husband to help in homeschooling. When he works at home, he has more time to spend with the children's learning, ideas, and general school related activities.

As we expanded our business, we realized the immense need for small businesses to create a successful online presence. Particularly homeschoolers who were side hustling as a way to make ends meet. However, often these side hustles can't afford "big business" web design and marketing plans. Our passion to homeschool our children has created a desire to see other homeschoolers succeed. Because of this, our company has morphed into an opportunity to help other homeschoolers get their businesses running efficiently. We see the immense need, and we willingly answer the call to help other parents to be successful.

Not every business starts with something you're already doing. God had given my husband his gift and passion for web design and business consulting long before we decided to make it a formal, organized operation. Sometimes businesses can begin out of a simple need, even if it's unchartered territory for you.

When I started a sewing pattern business in 2005, it was out of necessity. At that time, we were low on money and had a brand new baby. We didn't have much wiggle room for groceries, and disposable diapers were an added bill that I couldn't swallow. I purchased a sewing machine at a garage sale and began to design cloth diapers.

I had never sewn a thing in my life, and I needed to ask my mom for help to turn on the sewing machine. Yet, I was determined to design a cloth diaper for my baby that would save me money. As it turns out, I love to sew! I had no idea that creating something from cloth could be so fun. After countless failures and weeks later, I finally had a design that I loved. Back then, there weren't thousands of Pinterest ideas for how to DIY cloth diapers. I knew that I could help others if I made my designs available somewhere. That meant that I needed to learn how to use pattern designing software to draw my designs.

Learning how to run pattern designing software took me out of my element, and it was frustrating at times. The learning process was slow, but worth it! I made many mistakes, but with persistence, I was able to successfully make my first sewing pattern. Months after I had a successful design, I published my first sewing pattern of cloth diapers. I put it for sale on eBay (eBay was the most prominent platform at that time). In minutes, the pattern started selling. Now I was able to diaper my baby, and I started to cover my grocery bill.

Once I saw the cloth diaper patterns' success, I learned how to design clothing, and my business took off. My sewing pattern business is an excellent example of how you can start a business from a need, and watch it turn into something you love!

Owning your own business creates the need to act, regardless of our feelings or attitude.

My sewing pattern business is still active today, and I still like to design every once in a while. When I need a new outfit, or want to try a new style, I love to create it myself and make a new pattern design. My customers love it, and it keeps my mind sharp.

When you decide on a home business idea or are working your current business, you want to give it your very best. That's easiest to do when it's something that you genuinely enjoy. It's even more enjoyable to do if it helps others.

The Bible says in Colossians 3:23, "Whatever you do, work heartily, as for the Lord and not for men…" (ESV).

Genuinely doing our best when we work means doing it for the Lord and not for ourselves. If we have a business that makes other's lives better, we will be content. We will strive for excellence.

Willingness

Owning your own business is hard work; it requires careful planning and makes your home life devoted to work life. It makes your children and spouse part of your workday. In fact, if you homeschool, your children have the opportunity to become extensively involved in your work.

You're required to think creatively, which is a blessing but can also be overwhelming. Owning your own business creates the need to act, regardless of our feelings or attitude. The hardest part of owning a business is the willingness to work hard even on days we'd like to take a back seat.

Your business will thrive if you are willing to put in the time. It will succeed with the effort that you give it. When you are ready to commit effort, you gain momentum. Being willing isn't just an attitude. It isn't a feeling. It's a choice. Willingness comes from the desire to "make it work." When you are willing to do anything to make your business succeed, then succeed, you will.

> 2 Thessalonians 3:10 says, "…'If anyone is not willing to work, let him not eat.'"

If I rephrase this verse into a positive sense, it would say, "If you are willing to work, you will be able to eat."

My sister, Rebekah, used to be a nurse in a pediatric clinic. After she had children, she desired to be home with them and became a creative assistant for health and wellness companies. She designs art and graphics for her clients to use on their websites, social media, or newsletters. She creates newsletters and e-mails, manages social media, and a plethora of other tasks.

When she began her business, she was willing to put in the time to learn more graphic design skills. She was willing to help others at a minimal fee while she was learning. She desired to work solely with health and wellness companies, but she needed to be willing to work with other genres to get her business off the ground.

Rebekah saw her heart's desire and what she was good at. She was aiming for her goals, even when she was willing to work with other companies. Sometimes the ability to get to our goal will require the willingness to step outside our comfort zone. Be willing to work hard in and out of your comfort zones. Being open to getting out of your comfort zone will help you to achieve your goals.

When you work at home, you can be open to any circumstance. You have the freedom to change direction or make milestones along the way. By working at home, you can choose your path and achieve the goals that you set. There is so much freedom and satisfaction in setting a goal and achieving it.

Independence

When you work for yourself, you are responsible for yourself. You are responsible for paying your business bills, getting work done, hitting deadlines, and increasing customer satisfaction. You determine when and where you will work, and what hours you will do it. You will evaluate who you work with and what the purpose is in that business relationship.

When you work for yourself, you are in control of the budget and have a clear idea of how healthy your business is doing.

> "Aspire to live quietly, and mind your own affairs, and work with your hands, as we instructed you, so that you may walk properly before outsiders and be dependent on no one" (1 Thessalonians 4:11–12, ESV).

When I see verses like this, it makes me think that God desires us not to depend on other people all the time. We are to live quietly, mind our own business, work with our hands, and sometimes we can support ourselves.

Working for others can have excellent opportunities for benefits. However, sometimes employers don't offer benefits to their employees. By working at home, you can provide your own benefits. You could decide to pay off your home, or beef up your health insurance. You can also have more control over where your retirement account is held and managed.

More Opportunities

If you work for yourself, you have many opportunities that you wouldn't have working at an "outside of the home" job. Here are a couple of my favorite aspects:

Homeschool your children and watch them grow.

This is my number one reason to work at home. During a difficult financial period in my life, I spent a couple of years working outside of the home. It devastated me because I felt that my place was to be a homeschooling, and always present mother.. Instead, I was sending my children to public school and away from home sixty hours a week (forty hours plus drive time).

Some people don't have the option to work from home. I have lived in this situation myself for a time. However, if you have the option, consider working for yourself, or remotely, so that you won't miss any precious moments.

If you are interested in homeschooling, this is MUCH easier to do if you are working from home. Homeschooling can be done if you work outside of the home, but it can be straining on your children and people who help you in this area.

If you are interested in homeschooling but still need an established income, consider working at home.

You get to do what you love.

Have you ever had a job that you hated? You had to stay at it because it paid the bills, but it made you miserable? When you work for someone else, there will always be someone else's instructions for you to do. When you work for yourself, you get to choose to do what you love. The parts that you don't enjoy, you can hire out or possibly avoid altogether!

You don't have caps on creativity.

When you are working for someone else, there will always be the "mundane." Yet, the ordinary can allow you to think creatively and strategically when you are working for yourself. You never have that opportunity if you are fulfilling a position and its requirements for someone else.

Keeping to yourself.

I love to spend time with people. Sometimes. There are also days when I would rather stay at home, in my pajamas, and not be bothered. By working for yourself, you have the opportunity to decide who you spend time with.

If you want to spend time with a client, you have that choice. If you're going to spend time talking with your marketing team, you have that choice. If you decide to cancel your appointments and go to the beach, you can do that too.

It's not a hermit lifestyle we aim for, but the freedom to choose for yourself who you spend your time with.

You don't have financial caps.

What if you woke up one day and wanted to take a vacation to the Bahamas? Could you imagine a homeschool field trip like that?! Would you have the money sitting aside for you to do it? If you own your own business, you can decide to work more to save for that vacation. You could have a flash sale. You could go live on Facebook and make a live sale. You could make an extra batch of soap. You could do some additional marketing and get more clients. You could host a Lularoe party.

Whatever your money-making business is, you can do more of it when you need to. If you work for someone else, you are capped by what they allow you to work.

Raising your children with business skills.

Your kids are your shadow—they do what you do. They will think about what you think and go where you go. If you own a business while they are young, they will likely go in the same direction. If you are learning, they are learning. If you do your business with willingness, they will too. If you do whatever it takes to reach your goals, they will too. Your tenacity will be gifted to them. Raise your children while you run your business. This will give them business-minded skills that you'll be demonstrating to them. Then they can apply these skills to whatever career that they choose.

Wisdom

When you build your own business, you are starting a new chapter in life as a whole. You are creating something from nothing. When you make something, you want to build it in wisdom.

In any job that I've ever worked outside of the home, some careless people work there. When carelessness and foolishness enter a business, it becomes like a weed with a deep root. You can pull the weed, but there will be another plant that springs up somewhere else. No matter how much you dig the root, it still somehow survives. This scenario is typical of any job and can even become an issue in your own business. It is easy to get caught up in the weeds ourselves. We lose ourselves sometimes and forget the wisdom that we know to be true.

When you begin your businesses, you are weed-free. There isn't foolishness and carelessness. You have fertile soil from the beginning.

Proverbs 24:3–4 says, "By wisdom a house is built, and by understanding it is established; by knowledge the rooms are filled with all precious and pleasant riches" (NKJV).

Take your time to plan things well and to find competent counsel.

I want to encourage you to seek wisdom. Do not let foolishness and carelessness into your home and business. Take your time to plan things well and to find competent counsel. Do not throw money at everything or begin down paths that seem fishy. The future of a business that is built with wisdom and understanding "is established." That means that it will succeed.

Loving Others

When you own your own business, you have more opportunities to love others and use their gifts to push your business forward. I discuss this more in detail later, but I want you to have a general view of it now.

We all have natural gifts given to us by God. There are many natural gifts and many spiritual gifts. However, just like our fingerprints are different, our range of gifts can also be different. On top of gifts, you have different likes and dislikes. You also have tendencies and habits. All of these things make you into a unique person that God wants to use to accomplish amazing things.

> 1 Peter 4:10, "As each has received a gift, use it to serve one another, as good stewards of God's varied grace" (ESV).

1 Corinthians 13 is the quintessential passage of Scripture about love. In this chapter, we find a list of what love is. This chapter is talking about love, but it's deeper than that. What this chapter is really saying is that anything outside of love is void. It's worthless. God wants us to be so focused on love that we naturally become loving.

When we are doing something that is focused on loving, we stop being so consumed with "me, me, me, me." To gain traction in your business, while being balanced in every area of your life, you must look outside of your own four walls and let yourself be a little bit vulnerable while loving others.

> 1 Corinthians 12:7, "A spiritual gift is given to each of us so we can help each other" (NLT).

Because I am a homeschooler, along with a business owner, I am very mindful of incorporating other homeschoolers into my business or family needs.

For instance, as a large family, we eat a lot of produce. Instead of getting every apple at the grocery store, our family prefers to support a local, homeschooling fruit farm. Not only have we developed a friendship with these farmers, but we have helped to support their business. Supporting their business helps to support their homeschool. On top of these reasons, by purchasing fruit from these farmers, they deliver it directly to my doorstep. This saves me time that I can spend on my business instead of grocery shopping.

Another instance that I use homeschoolers to propel my business is to outsource projects to other homeschoolers. As our Web Agency grows, sometimes we need to hire additional help. We purposefully make "help wanted" ads for homeschoolers, and work with them remotely. This helps them to support their family, and we are able to utilize their incredible gifts in our business. Sometimes the rates might be more costly, but by putting love first, rather than a dollar, we can affect more lives positively.

Consider helping other homeschoolers while utilizing their gifts and services to help you propel your business forward. When you support other homeschoolers, you are helping them stay at home with their children. You are helping them survive this crazy world and to train their kids in moral values. You can support homeschoolers by hiring them to do projects and tasks for you. If you are hired by another homeschooler, use this as an opportunity to love someone by using your gifts to help them.

Points to Ponder:

What am I good at?

What needs can I fill?

What would independence instead of a job do in my life?

What opportunities will I or do I have with my own business?

What are the areas of foolishness or carelessness that I could fall into with my business?

What are the areas in my business that I need wisdom?

What are some ways that I can help others use their gifts?

Chapter Eight

Business

Business has always come naturally to me. I enjoy the entire process—from the dreaming, creating, sales, fulfilling, and even the financial recording.

As a middle schooler, I would ask fellow church-goers if they needed date nights so that I could babysit. When we would have youth group fundraisers, I always raised more money than other kids my age—I had no fear of sales.

As soon as I had my driver's license, I was working multiple jobs and teaching piano lessons. Coordinating high school and three jobs was a challenge, but it taught me many things about time management at an early age.

After high school graduation, I continued with multiple jobs, but I also began to teach myself guitar. I was certain that if I was successful at piano lessons, than I could be successful at guitar lessons too. Funny enough, my idea worked! In no time, I had six guitar students that I was teaching while I was learning myself.

When my first baby was born, I began to design sewing patterns. I'll tell you more about this story soon. As an adult, this has been a business that I can keep coming back to when I need a creative outlet (or a new blouse). It is still running successfully sixteen years later.

As a homeschooling mother myself, I have begun to support other homeschoolers and families by building websites with our family web agency. It is such a blessing to put others first in this way, and to support others who have the same vision for their families as we do.

This list is only a small snippet of the business ventures that I have started or have been a part of. However, even if they weren't successful, each experience has taught me valuable lessons. Lessons in relationships, strengths and weaknesses, and determination have shaped the way I think about life in general. It's important to see each of your experiences as a life lesson. Each situation, whether in life or business, is an opportunity to grow your character.

Careful organization is what makes my businesses successful.

In each of my businesses, I loved the freedom that it gave me to have "my own thing." Building organized workspaces and coordination of clients is exciting to me, so I feel like my business is my "freedom" so to speak. Many women like to get their nails done, or to have a ladies night out— give me two hours of business time, and I'm a happy camper.

I have learned that careful organization is what makes my businesses successful. I work more efficiently when I know where my tools are. It's the same in the office—if you know where your "work tools" are, and if you are organized in your planning, you will be more efficient.

Planning for clients and deadlines are not different. Keeping a strict and written schedule has saved me from many disappointments. In fact, I prefer to give extra time than needed for each project.

For instance, I recently had a client that wanted a web launch as soon as I could get it done. Instead of telling her that I could launch in one week (which I could), I gave the project a three-week deadline. There were some details that I wasn't aware of in the building process, and the entire project took 10 days. This customer was extremely happy that I was able to give her an early launch! Even though I could have projected my deadline to be ready in one week, by giving myself extra time in the project, it allowed me to avoid the stress of a missed deadline. When you plan and coordinate deadlines, give yourself some buffer room so that you don't disappoint your customers.

By starting, building, or continuing businesses, I have learned to appreciate each moment of difficulty as well. Difficult times seem to be the moments when a person learns the most. I have found this to be true in my own life. In fact, where I live is a rural area in which most people have similar social backgrounds and beliefs. By being a business owner online, I have had experiences with people that I have nothing in common with, who I don't understand, and who can to be difficult to work with. This is much different than I experience in my local environment. This has helped me grow as a person in ways that I never would have been able to if I was to stay in my local, comfortable environment. The lessons that I have learned from each of these experiences stick in my mind and create better character. Never let negative feedback or disgruntled clients destroy your vision. Instead, learn from each circumstance and decide how to handle it differently next time.

Recently I was checking my email for my sewing pattern business. I had a customer who left a poor review of my website because they couldn't get an expired coupon to work. The review had nothing to do with my pattern, or website, but because they couldn't use an expired coupon. Instead of being frustrated about this, I am looking at it in a new way: What if I didn't have expiration dates on my coupons? People seldom use coupons anyway, so I wouldn't be out anything if someone used it. I would have happy customers, and less work to deal with negative comments.

This is how I use negative feedback to my advantage. There are many people who want to be your customer, and the ones who don't can still teach us something.

Whatever your job or title is, remember first that it's okay to try something new. And it's okay if it doesn't work. In fact, failure today might be what leads you to success tomorrow. Take each experience as deeper learning and forward movement, even if it isn't the outcome that you desire.

This book is the first one that I've ever written. Even as I write it, I am not sure if it will come of anything. Yet, my drive to help others is more important to me than the possibility of failure. The things that I have learned while putting together each page is beyond remarkable in the growing process. Even if this book doesn't get put on a shelf, the value that I have from the writing process is better than selling thousands of copies.

Regardless of what my job title is, my favorite place to work is at home. To me, if I'm still able to work at home, I'm successful. My family and my children are the reason for this. To homeschool my children and to help my husband in any way that I can is pure motivation for me. However, many parents find it difficult to imagine working at home, and maybe aren't even sure how to begin. If that's you, I have so much to discuss with you. If your desire is to work at home, but if you aren't sure where to start, I want to ease your mind. If you've been working at home for a while, hopefully I'll spur some new ideas along the way.

Since I love the business creation process, let's even take a look at your foundations of why you would want to work at home.

Points to Ponder:

What are you naturally gifted at?

Was there anything in your life recently which was negative?

How can you look at the negative as a way to improve yourself?

What is your reason for reading this book?

Chapter Nine

Homeschooling 101

In the past few months, I have been asked countless times about my homeschool. The parents who are asking are usually parents who have kicked around homeschooling before, but have never gotten serious about it until a pandemic affected our country and schools.

I have had people sit across from me at my kitchen table, asking me, "How can I fit homeschool into my busy life?" Or "How can I run a business successfully while homeschooling?" The most important question though, is, "How do I get started with homeschooling?"

I must tell you that I am far from all knowledgeable on the subject of homeschooling. In this section, I will share my personal homeschool goals, and what I believe to be important when getting started. I will also share what works best in our household, but don't be afraid to try something different. I'll do my best to explain why I choose to do certain things. Please remember that every family is different, and each child learns differently. What works for me might not work for you. However, let this be a starting point for your homeschool journey.

Now, come sit at my kitchen table and let's chat a while...

Define the Purpose of Homeschooling

Before we get into the nitty gritty details of homeschooling, we need to start at the beginning. If you are going to successfully homeschool, you need to have a reason why you are homeschooling. There will be days you want to throw in the towel, and your reason is what you will need to come back to. The reason for homeschooling should be a moral one. I feel this way because your decision needs to depend on you…not on other people. Let me explain by giving you an example.

Sally has always sent her daughter, Samantha, to public school. She has contemplated homeschooling before, but it wasn't a huge priority until now.

Lately, Sally feels like Samantha isn't getting the proper education that she needs. Even though Samantha is a grade A student, she frequently feels bored while waiting for her classmates to catch up. Samantha's teacher does her best in the class, but with the state's requirements, she is limited in what she can teach. This also limits her ability to challenge Samantha in school. On top of all of this, there are some nasty kids in Samantha's class that are gossiping and bullying.

Sally knows that she can homeschool her daughter, and that she can give her more opportunities at home. She knows that God calls us to "train our children when they are young, and when they are old, they will not depart from it" (Proverbs 22:6). However, up until this point, she has been satisfied with the school system. After great pondering, Sally makes the decision to remove Samantha from the public school and to homeschool her.

Why did Sally pull Samantha out of school? Was it because the teacher wasn't challenging her? Was the gossiping and the bullying the final reason? Nope.

Sally's reason for homeschooling must be a decision that she makes herself…without the comparison of others. Sally's decision to homeschool needs to be the framed in a way that is positive toward herself and her abilities:

Sally knows that she can teach Samantha school while moving her ahead in the areas that she excels in. Sally is not limited in her teaching and knows that she can round Samantha's education by giving her more variety than the public school has access to. Sally wants to give Samantha friendship opportunities with like-minded families. She ultimately decides to homeschool because she feels that is her calling by God to teach her children.

Like Sally, you need to make the decision to homeschool based on yourself. Your morals. Your ability to teach, the opportunities that you will offer your children. Do not choose to homeschool based on failure of the school system or discrepancy of others. Your decision to homeschool should not be formed by the negative attributes of what you are leaving. You will never be truly content in your homeschool, life, or business if you feel that you need to always "do better" than the one that failed. You will feel completely confident when you make a decision based on yourself.

Another reason you want to make a "reason for homeschooling" is the state may change your rights if you do not have a good reason. At the time of writing this book, COVID-19 is possibly going to affect the school systems in the United States drastically. In a world that is constantly changing, we need to have a plan. Our Freedom of Religion in the Bill of Rights is a good battle plan. Here's an example.

Vaccines can be a controversial subject for many families. Whether you agree or disagree with vaccines, did you know that many states require vaccinations of all children? In most of these states, the only way you can get a vaccination waiver is a letter from your doctor, or because of religion. Your Freedom of Religion may eventually save the day in regards to homeschool too.

I recommend that you base your reason to homeschool primarily on a religious reason. I strongly suggest having a few Bible verses included in your "reason to homeschool" as well.

Another great reason to homeschool is if your child has special needs. I personally know a couple of families who homeschool simply because of the special needs of their children. They want to see their children getting personalized education and stimulation they require. No institution can provide every need of every child. You know what your child needs best.

Because of special needs, you may also get a written recommendation from a doctor, which will help your case to homeschool if you are ever required to carry this documentation.

When you write your "reason to homeschool", type it out, and maybe even frame it on the wall. There will be days when you need to read it. There will be moments when you will wonder, "why on earth did I ever agree to this?!" During those moments, you will thank me for telling you to write the document. You're welcome, mama.

Protection

Children are incredible learners. According to science, they are like learning sponges at a young age. For this reason, our society has placed education on a pedestal for young people. Because of this, there are also laws in place that protect children from being kept away from a formal education.

Children are incredible learners.

Homeschoolers tend to be watched more carefully because of these laws. This isn't a problem if you have proper protection in place. In fact, homeschooling is incredibly accepted in 2020 as compared to twenty years ago. However, there are still the small minority who believe that parents do not have any business educating their children.

Child protective services (CPS) was designed to keep children safe. Since its origin, they have protected many children from precarious situations. Homeschooling is typically not a valid reason to have CPS involved; however, there are people (or neighbors) who think that calling CPS is doing society a favor.

If CPS gets called about your homeschool, they will likely want to do an "audit" of your schooling practices. In this circumstance, you will need to provide documents and statements regarding homeschooling your children.

Most parents believe that CPS will give the benefit of the doubt for your homeschool, and for the good of your home and lifestyle. Unfortunately, sometimes parents are taken by surprise when a disgruntled state employee sees the home negatively. Some parents are even taken to court and required to jump through hoops to keep their children safe from removal. Sometimes these cases are legitimate; however, I have read a plethora of stories where it isn't. In these cases, some parents' rights become trampled if they are not legally protected.

Please don't be afraid; CPS is not a reason to avoid homeschooling. You simply need legal support. Almost like homeschool insurance. There is an absolute blessing of an organization called "Homeschool Legal Defense Association," or HSLDA. It is an organization that you pay membership to every year, and you get a phone number to call in the event you are audited by the state. If CPS calls or knocks, you call the lawyer on the card to do any speaking for you. They will protect you and your family with anything law-related. Become a member of HSLDA and have peace of mind in this area.

The HSLDA recommends that you keep certain documents and files to also prepare for a state audit. These are simple steps that you can prepare easily, once or twice a year, just to give yourself some extra insurance.

1. Be a good record-keeper.

Keep a record of your child's grades, special projects, achievements, and awards. These show that they are being schooled and socialized. Tracking these records throughout the year will keep you from being stressed as you finish your grading projects. Once your file is full, you can close the school year.

2. Write a yearly plan.

Each year, write a plan for every child in your homeschool. Write the subjects you will be teaching them, and what you hope to accomplish with them. Write how many days you plan to do school, and any field trips that you know you'll take.

3. Narrations for older children.

If you have children in third grade and older, have them write subject narrations at the end of the year. I typically will have my children write a one- or two-page essay for each subject or interest that they had that year. If they worked a job, or if they studied something on their own, I also have them write a narration for that. For instance, my daughter who loves history went through a phase of listening to podcasts about historical figures. She made a lovely narration of a compilation of people she learned about. My other daughter began a job of photo editing and customer service. She had to learn various computer programs to accomplish the job, so she wrote a narration for the job. Basically, anything that is educational, they should write a narration about at the end of the school year. This is perfect to include in your record-keeping file.

4. Become a member of a Co-op.

A co-op is a group of homeschoolers who get together for classes or events on a regular basis. They are typically a parent-run program and have memberships for which you must apply and be approved. Since homeschooling is becoming more common, co-ops are in most cities. It is unlikely that there isn't at least one homeschool co-op in your area. Look online for one to join. Often there are classes or even field trips these groups do together. By joining a local co-op, you will have the advantage of being affiliated with a larger homeschool community and group. You will get local homeschool news and events, as well as be recognized by others in the area. Although this doesn't seem like a safety procedure, it shows the state that you are actively participating in a community. The state will prefer you if you are affiliated with a group. Regardless of the state, you and your children will love the opportunities that co-ops offer for socialization. I'll go more into detail later.

5. Calendar or journal everything.

I have two calendars. I have my everyday calendar, and I have my business calendar. Many, many, many parents have a homeschool planner, but I am not that girl. As a business owner, and juggling many different things, I certainly don't need one more calendar to fill out.

In my everyday calendar, I write down everything. If I have a dentist appointment, I write it down. If we unexpectedly go to a friend's house, I add it to the calendar. I write down how many days we are in school (many states require 180 days). If we haul wood for a grandparent, I write it down. If my teen has a work schedule, I write it down. Anything that could be counted as medical, learning, socialization, or community service, I write it in the calendar. This way, if I was ever audited, I have a very detailed list of their socialization, and how many days they've been in school.

In Chapter 2: Structure, I discussed how to keep the calendar. It's an excellent way to keep track of homeschool and your entire home. Make sure that you don't miss these amazing tips.

Requirements

Homeschool requirements are different in each state. When you become a member of the HSLDA, you will be given multiple resources. One of these resources is a list of requirements of your state. I live in Michigan, which is a very lenient state, and the tiny list of homeschool requirements are very vague. Because of the vague laws, it leaves a lot to be interpreted. Although many parents find the vagueness to be freeing in their homeschool, I want to make sure that my family is prepared for any situation. Since there is wiggle room in the text of the law, I try to make sure that I am fully following it by going beyond the requirements.

Even though Michigan has few laws regarding what subjects to teach, and they don't require me to keep records as I do, I keep significant records anyway. I also try to make sure that my children are following the same class schedule as their peers in public school. For instance, public schools require teenagers to take Algebra 1 and 2, Geometry, and another higher learning math program in high school. Michigan public schools have multiple credit requirements that are not required for homeschool programs. I follow the requirements of the public school so my children are at pace with their peers. When I plan my children's high school, I carefully map out all four years for them, so they will take all public school required classes. I strongly recommend that when you enter into high school years, you take the time to map out their entire high school. This will give you a plan that you won't need to think about later.

Colleges also have some requirements to consider. Most colleges and trade schools are welcoming to homeschoolers, but it's always a good idea to check with potential colleges of interest.

Many times, colleges still want an SAT or ACT test. These tests are typically taken in the junior and senior years of high school. They cost a minimal fee, and any school-age child can take them.

You'll find information for these testing opportunities by doing a simple Google search. Plan ahead for these when you are planning your school year. You don't want to get caught off-guard. A simple way to being a successful businesswoman and homeschooling mom is having a solid plan. This will help you keep balance.

Some parents are concerned about requirements in state-level testing. In my state, it isn't required at this time, but it is required in many other states. Research the guidelines for your state and make the plan to take state testing if necessary. Write it in the calendar and don't fret. If it isn't required in your state, I wouldn't bother to take the state tests. In my opinion, all it does is invite state input into your home, and I think that is unnecessary stress.

Alternatively, if you want to check the grade level of your children, there are many curricula which have a "placement test" for placing your children into the proper grade. Feel free to utilize these programs, but again, don't fret. I don't use them. Every curriculum teaches information at different stages and levels. I try to keep my children in the grade level or above grade level as their peers. If a child is struggling to keep up in one area, consider adding supplemental resources at that time until the child is solid.

Socialization

I'm sure you've heard the myth that homeschooled kids aren't as prepared socially as peers in traditional schools. This is not true! Some of the sweetest, and most well-mannered children are homeschooled. They have excellent conversations and social skills. My children are confident speakers, and enjoy conversing with whomever they meet.

It's incredibly important to spend time talking with your children. Speak with them like they are intelligent human beings. They are!

Include them in your adult conversations, and don't try to "dumb down" your speech when they are around.

Talking with your children intelligently, including them in adult conversation, and expecting their mature response is where they will learn the best social skills. Do not expect that "outside sources" will teach your children to socialize better than you can. In fact, use socialization as a way to get a "temperature" of the social skills of your child.

Regardless of the age of your children, it's very important that you find other homeschoolers as a "home base." Being able to bounce ideas off of other moms and seeing them interact with their children are great ways you can learn. Going to my local co-op has been an excellent way for me to connect with other parents.

Many co-ops have classes available for parents to volunteer or charge to teach classes. The co-op classes are meant for the children; however, adult relationships thrive during this time. Troubleshooting tough courses, curriculum ideas, and getting new ideas are only a few things that are beneficial for parents when you can be a member of a co-op.

Being able to bounce ideas off of other moms and seeing them interact with their children are great ways you can learn.

Many local co-ops also do field trips together. Similarly to public schools, homeschoolers can get group rates, group tours, and special passes that are not available to the public. Oftentimes, co-op groups ask for field trip ideas, so keep a list of the places you'd like to share with your children.

Field trips are a fantastic way to be involved in a co-op, even if you don't have a "class day." Your children will develop friendships with you close by, and they will have great learning experiences with other children. By taking advantage of field trips through a local homeschool co-op, you can expand your children's scope and experiences.

If co-ops aren't your thing, or if they don't fit in your schedule, you can also get your children involved in various interest groups. Groups and classes such as music, theater, sports, martial arts, swim, and gym classes are available in many communities. The diverse array of people who attend are an added benefit of interest groups for your kids. Use this type of experience for your child to develop relationships with children and adults of all ages and backgrounds.

By encouraging your children to work or to make a business of their own, it gives them ownership and pride.

Many churches also offer various groups that are available for children. For instance, Mothers Of Preschoolers (MOPS) is a nationwide program in which many churches participate. MOPs groups often meet during the daytime, and have child care available. Even though MOPS is for mothers, the children usually are spending time playing, doing crafts, and generally socializing.

For older children, consider checking out some youth groups in your community. Many churches have youth programs in which Christian teenagers get together to build friendships and learn more about faith. This is a great opportunity for your kids to build relationships within the church.

Another option, and one of my favorite ways to get my children socialized, is to allow them to work at a job. By encouraging your children to work or to make a business of their own, it gives them ownership and pride. This type of socialization also allows your children to be around others who are working toward the same goal. You will find that a job will encourage your child to pursue excellent work ethics, and teach them the value of working hard.

For children who are too young to have a paying job, consider setting up an internship with a trusted adult who has a hobby or occupation that interests your child. Many children are interested to learn things that their parents are not knowledgeable about. By allowing your child to study from a new perspective, there is more opportunity for learning.

Curriculum

In this section, I am offering my personal experience in regards to curriculum. Please remember that many families are different, and what works for me may not be the best for your family. However, I have had great success with the choices I have made. The curriculum options I choose allow me to balance homeschooling five children and run my business successfully.

Self-Lead Learning

When you are running a business, a home, training your children, and homeschooling, you need time. You absolutely can't waste a single moment. What I have found profoundly helpful is teaching my children to "self-teach". Self-lead learning isn't a new thing. In fact, if you think back to when schools were K-12 in one room, the children couldn't all wait on their teacher for everything. They had to do their work on their own. Self-lead learning in the home is similar. Starting as soon as the child is holding a writing utensil, give them instruction, and walk away. Start this in small increments. You will feel like you are getting nowhere for a while, but it will sink in. I promise you.

After a time of walking away for a few minutes at a time, start to increase your time away. Give your child freedom to go ahead in their coloring books or workbooks. Encourage children who work by themselves without help. If they need your help, come to them for a short time and walk away again. This begins the habit of self-lead learning very early in your homeschooling.

If your child has been in public school before or is an older child, this process is much easier to begin. However, it may be something you still have to train. Be consistent. Walk away. If a child needs help in an area, and you cannot come right away, allow them to skip the problem and to move on. This solidifies in the mind of a child that they are capable of learning without your help. By the way, if you haven't read the Parenting chapter in this book, don't miss out. I discuss training in significant detail.

Self-lead learning is crucial to a mother with multiple children and to the business owner. You simply cannot sit every second beside your children while they learn. It's not healthy for them, as they need to process and think for themselves. It's also not healthy for you, as you'll be stressing about all the things you need to get done.

When you are picking a curriculum, try to choose easy to understand material that does not require the teacher's constant supervision. If you must get a teacher's manual, chances are this is not a self-lead learning style of a curriculum.

Mastery vs. Spiral Learning

As your child progresses through school, you'll find lessons repeating themselves. You'll learn about the same presidents, the same history lessons, the same science lessons, and language lessons. Repeating is important because it solidifies precepts in your child's mind. As they get older, they will delve deeper into the subjects. Each time they learn about something, it will come with more information and they will learn more about it. This is common across all curricula.

Math curricula have a different approach: Mastery and Spiral. Allow me to introduce you to each concept so you will give your children the opportunity for success in math.

Mastery

Mastery-style math programs are what we grew up with prior to 2005. When you think of how you were taught addition, then subtraction, then multiplication, then division, it is mastery—the student "masters" a concept before proceeding to the next, more challenging step. A student spends countless days doing drills and flashcards. A student does worksheet after worksheet, and when they have completed the section, they are confident and sure-footed in the subject. Mastery doesn't leave much room for variety from day to day and can be boring for some students.

I prefer mastery curricula for math because it requires less of my intervention and teaching time. It allows my kids to do more lessons on their own, without my help. If I am going to be successful at running my home, teaching school, and running a business, time is something to be saved. My favorite math program for 3–8 grade is called Strayer Upton. It's very old-fashioned, but it is thorough and student paced. Unfortunately, this program is not self-grading. However, choosing mastery programs, gives me a balanced approach to teaching math to my children.

Spiral

Many curricula are starting to embrace spiral math. You can think of spiral math like a spring or slinky. As you go up the spring, you are gaining momentum, but at a slower rate. The children will learn a little about this, and a little of that. The school work will seem below grade level in some cases, but in other cases, you feel that they are beyond their grade.

When we began our homeschool journey, I began with a spiral curriculum. It was very difficult for my children, which made it difficult for me. They struggled to remember everything they had been taught, only to introduce a new concept the next day. Because they didn't master a concept, there wasn't much practice, and I had to supplement the curriculum often. This required more thinking time and research on my part.

Many parents and children love the variety of spiral math programs. A favorite math program among my homeschool friends is Teaching Textbooks. It automatically grades and is very user friendly.

However, in my home, I need to be more hands-off than a spiral math program allows. This should be carefully considered as you choose a math curriculum.

The Littles and the Bigs

In my home, we have a vast gap between two "sets" of children. We have the Littles and we have the Bigs. My Littles are ages three, five, and seven. My Bigs are fifteen and sixteen years old. It's important that you recognize each age set of children have similarities, but they also have different needs in your homeschooling.

Littles

Children who are younger than third grade are so much fun. This is the most impressionable time of their learning and when the joy of learning can manifest. They learn to read and they start to gobble up books. During this time, I find fun books they are interested in and let them pour over them. It's okay if they aren't classic books, and it's okay if there is a couple of pictures in the book. The point is for them to develop a love for reading. My seven-year-old is reading a set of dragon books right now. The subject matter is definitely not my style, but the books are clean reading, and her vocabulary is exploding!

Many parents struggle with their children not wanting to read. However, if you get the books they are excited to read, and you encourage them to read, and even schedule a time for them to read, they will blossom.

Littles are easy to purchase curriculum for as well. I typically find workbooks on Amazon for any children who are below third grade. This is affordable and also a great way for children to have a sense of ownership as the books are generally easy to maneuver with self-lead learning. I love the depth of Christian curricula that have amazing options. However, for young students, I have discovered that Spectrum or 180 Days brands are absolutely perfect.

Remember to check with your homeschool state laws to see

what subjects you need to teach. It's important that you teach a well-rounded curriculum.

Please don't forget to get your child a good Bible program. A new favorite of mine is Bob Jones Video Learning for our Bible class. It's a video that guides the entire year of Bible class and all of my Littles can participate. That's a half-hour gained to take a shower or put some dinner on while the babies learn about Jesus. Perfect.

It's important that you teach a well-rounded curriculum.

Utilize programs that multiple children can share the learning together. For instance, The Bible program that I just mentioned is perfect for my Littles to do together. They can talk about it with each other and sit together to watch it. This encourages kindness with each other and friendship between them as well.

Another idea is to use audio programs for your children. An example of this would be listening to audiobooks on historical figures. Set the timer for thirty minutes, and you have an excellent history lesson that requires nothing of you. Some parents like to take this approach if they are spending time in a vehicle. I personally enjoy using this time as practice for them to sit still and listen intently. This year I ordered Story of the World as our history curriculum for the Littles. They love it, and it gives me a few minutes to get chores done. There are workbooks and tests available online for this audiobook. However, I choose to allow them to soak it all in at this age without the stress of a workbook for history. Another amazing audio option is "YWAM." They come on CDs or MP3s and they focus on historical figures in great detail.

Before third grade, you want to get your child familiar with a computer. This can be in the form of educational games (also saving time for you while keeping them busy), and typing practice. In third grade, most online and digital curricula become available, and you may want to take advantage of one. It'll change your homeschool for the better!

The final thing that I want to mention about Littles, and this might come as a shock: I don't keep daily lesson plans. At the beginning of the year, I write a plan as far as what books I'll be using and what the children are going to learn. However, when it comes to the day-to-day teaching, I don't write a plan.

Here's what I do instead:

At the beginning of the year, I make a weekly chart for each child. Each day of the week has a checklist of subjects to do. The children, who are self-directed learners, see what they need to do, go to the next page in their book, and they do it! I use the same chart for the entire year.

When you homeschool, things change all the time; someone gets sick, you go to the library instead of a history lesson, or any number of reasons plans will change. By not having a daily lesson plan, I am free to change up my homeschool as I need to. This was a huge area of stress that the Lord freed me from. I implore you: do not get bogged down by your school planner. It isn't healthy for you to stress about it.

Bigs

After third grade, things start to pick up in learning intensity. This is the time when math programs really start to "amp" up, and when online courses become available. By the time your child is in third grade, it's a good idea for them to know how to use a computer. They should have control over the mouse and have a general idea of where the keys are to type. They should also understand how to navigate through tabs on a browser and find things on the computer.

Once a child is older than third grade, this is where you will want to choose your math program carefully. You'll need to decide which direction you want to go. Once you start down mastery, it's best to stay with it. If you start down the spiral path, it's difficult to transition into mastery. However, it can be done—don't let me scare you. Remember, I started with spiral and went to mastery. It set us back a little at the time, but we caught up with a two-year plan.

In third grade, you'll also find the requirements of spelling and language arts programs increase for students. It's important during the third- and fourth-grade years to not go overboard with trying to do too much. You'll overwhelm your child and they could start to have a distaste for school. If you choose to try too many subjects or too many books, you'll get overwhelmed and not have time for your morning coffee, much less your business. This is not balanced.

By fifth grade, I would highly recommend you take advantage of some of the online programs that are available for parents. There are academies where a teacher will literally teach your children at home (these are extremely expensive). There are also more affordable parent-lead programs which self-grade their work.

The self-grading program I use is called "Monarch." It's easy for me, and it's a blessing for my children. I have to read and grade essays, but the program stores everything and does most of the grading tasks for me. The program sets up the children's daily tasks and you can adjust your schedule at any time. In fact, if you take off a day, it will recalibrate your lesson plans too! You won't have to touch a thing!

As your children's workload increases, I strongly suggest getting a self-guided program. Find a program that does not include a teacher's manual. A self-grading program is best. Our homeschool opportunities in 2020 are incredible. Please use the wonderful resources available to us, so you can stay at home with your children and run your home business.

Something else to think about with older children is the concept of open- or closed-book learning. When I was young, the schools used the closed-book method. "Closed book" is when a child has to memorize things for a test or quiz. Open book is when a child is allowed to find the answer in a book or on

Google.

Some people are preoccupied with teaching how to know from heart how to do everything, when in reality, a quick YouTube or Google search can provide the answers to nearly anything! I want my children to know how to find the answer to any question they have…not necessarily to know it all from the start.

The greatest thing you can give your child is the ability to know how to learn.

In my life as a successful adult, I use an open-book method. If I can't remember a fact, or if I need help to do an algebraic equation, I look it up on Google. I use this same method for teaching my children to be successful in life.

In fact, I use open books for tests and quizzes as well. This not only empowers them to get their school done well, but it allows them the same resources we have, as adults, in the real world.

The greatest thing you can give your child is the ability to know how to learn, and to find the answers that will make them successful. In my homeschool, I encourage my children to find the answer to their questions on their own. This not only drives them in their self-lead learning, but it also teaches them how to find answers without dependency on others. It teaches your children how easy it is to look it up in a book, or how easy it is to look it up online.

My disclaimer though? They aren't allowed to get less than ninety percent. In my opinion, there is no reason they should get anything wrong with the open-book method. If they get less than ninety percent, they are required to wipe the lesson and do the entire thing over again.

Another thing to consider in regards to the open-book method is our relationship with God.

> The Bible is God's Word, and 2 Timothy 3:16-17 says: "All Scripture is breathed out by God and profitable for teaching, for reproof, for correction, and for training in righteousness, that the man of God may be competent, equipped for every good work" (ESV).

As Christians, we are instructed to use the Bible to learn, teach, correct, and train. We are always allowed and encouraged to be reading the Bible as our source of truth.

> The Bible is an "open book" for us so "that the man of God may be competent" (2 Timothy 3:17).

I believe my school should take the same approach.

By having the open-book system in place, my children are incredible learners. They are well beyond their grade levels and retain much more knowledge than I ever did in high school.

On top of all that, it also gives me the ability to be nearly hands-off. It keeps me from getting frustrated at them or feeling like we need to work on something a little more. If they don't understand the lesson, they search their books, they watch videos, they read articles—anything to understand it. It's freeing to me and completely teaches my children in ways I never could. As you set up your homeschool, please consider allowing your children to use an open-book method. At least in part. You'll find their learning and confidence skyrockets.

School Files

Once you decide to homeschool, and keep records, you'll need a place to keep them. I buy plastic filing boxes with lids where I keep all of my children's things for each year. I also have a "master" box, in which I keep the extra important things I will discuss later.

Student Work Files

The "Student Work Files" are the files I work with each year. Each year gets a box, and all of the articles I keep for each child go into the box. Sometimes I keep entire workbooks in these files. It doesn't have to be a lot, but should be enough to show the state the progress the children have made if you were ever audited.

Important Files

This is a separate box that has our most important documents in it. I'm including some important documents I have in my important files. You may add more or less throughout your homeschooling adventure.

Cumulative Record Per Child

The Cumulative Record is a file folder that will allow you to keep track of your child's subjects and grades. It also has important school location information: address, contact information, academic record, and graduation date. If you pull your child out of public school, your children already have a cumulative record. You should get any files the public school has so you can add it to their individual file.

The Cumulative Record is also an excellent place to store awards and achievements your student has received. You can purchase these files on Amazon or ChristianBook.com.

Reason for Homeschooling

As we discussed earlier in this chapter, it is important to have a reason for homeschooling written and signed. Keep a copy of this document in your important files.

HSLDA Paperwork

The HSLDA will give you a phone number and information

to call if there is ever an issue with the school system or state. It is important to always keep the most updated copy of your HSLDA membership available. This is also an excellent place to keep any state requirements you've printed.

High School Plan

If you have high schoolers, you'll want to have a plan mapped out for them in regards to what classes they will be taking so they can get all the credits required. This is a good idea to keep in this box, or in the cumulative record of the child.

School Year Goals

Each school year, you will make goals and plan for your homeschool. It's a good idea to put it in their Cumulative folder. Many families choose to do one document instead of individual student goals. This would need to be saved in the important files as well.

Your child inherently wants to please you, so show them how they can help you.

Using Business to Enhance Learning

If you are a business owner or are soon to be a business owner, it's a wise idea to include your children in your work. This will help them understand your goals and how important it is that they do their part. Your child inherently wants to please you, so show them how they can help you.

When your children see that you love something, or are passionate about your business, they will want to be involved. Sometimes, they might not be crazy about the process, but will come to enjoy being part of the family business. They will feel included and needed. On top of that, to include your children in your business also means you can get more work done. I've included a small list of ideas your children can help you with. This is very small, and can't compare to the infinite options you can dream up for your children.

Typing Projects

Remember what I said about typing? By the time your child is in third grade, you can have them type projects or notes for you. This is an excellent skill and helpful for you! Simply have them type out your handwritten notes, or have them write some reviews. You'll be surprised at how well they take to such tasks. Not only is this excellent practice at typing and gathering information, but it is also an opportunity for language skills, spelling, and grammar.

Organizing

We discussed structure and organizing in Chapter 2, but are you aware that your children can and should be helping you organize? Whether you are having Littles organize your buttons, or your Bigs organizing your product photos, this is an excellent way to involve your children.

Article Writing

An excellent way older children can improve their language and writing skills is to have them write articles for your business. It's a learning curve, but absolutely worth putting the effort into teaching.

Idea-Forming

Littles and Bigs enjoy this practice so much you'll need to take notes! Get your children involved in the brainstorm process. Encourage their goofy ideas as well as the impossible ones. Then discuss these ideas and see which ones would be a valuable asset to your business. What an amazing boost to your children to see their deas utilized in their family's business! We want our children to be creative and to make the impossible possible. This is so important to teach them, and your business is the perfect outlet for them to see it in practice.

Product-Making

Do you have a physical product you make and sell? Maybe you make soap, or jewelry, or clothes. Maybe you are a woodworker, or an artist. Regardless of what your business is, let your children work at it with you. Let them help you pour the soap. Let them help you organize the jewelry and string some beads. Let them help you sew a little and snip some strings. Regardless of your product, encourage and allow your children to be creative with you.

Product Packaging

If you ship goods, let your children help you print labels and package. This will make a tedious job much more fun, and give them a life skill.

Article and Information Learning

If your business requires a learning curve, give your children the tools that they will need to help you. For instance, if your business requires photo editing, have your child take an online class in Photoshop. If your business requires research, have your child do research for you!

Hired Jobs

I'll talk more about hiring jobs in Chapter 10: Gaining Traction, but I just want to insert a snippet here: Your kids need money and a paying job too. If you have older children who are capable of learning how to manage your Facebook, send e-mails, to manage Instagram or customer service, train and hire them to work for you. It will give them life skills and a wonderful way they can earn money while being part of the family business.

Homeschool Day-to-Day Structure

In Chapter 2: Structure, we discussed how to incorporate structure into your home. So what does a structured schedule look like? I know you're wondering how to fit it all in, so I wanted to write out a typical schedule I work with. Please feel free to modify my example to fit your own parenting style and children's needs.

6:00 a.m.

This is my time. I sip my coffee, read my Bible, and think. I have two notebooks with me; one is my "prayer" journal, and the other is my regular journal. I turn my regular journal to a new page and use it as a "thinking" page. I believe that I am most creative and clear-headed at this time of day.

My Bible reading and prayer will often spur some thoughts about business, so I want to have a separate place to write them down. This has proved to be the most valuable part of my day. I also like to write a small list of my plans for the day during this time. I discussed this at length in Chapter 4: Spiritual Health.

7:00 a.m.

This is my Bigs' time to get up. They stay in their room or bathroom. They have reading time to themselves, and also get ready for the day. This is also when I get myself prepared for the day and do anything that I need to do before little feet hit the ground.

8:00 a.m.

This is when the Littles come out of their rooms. They brush their teeth, start their morning chores, and everyone gathers for breakfast. During breakfast, we discuss the day's events and anything else that we need to have a family discussion about. Remember how I told you about the light-up clock? This clock is exactly how I taught my young children to stay in their beds until eight.

8:30–9:00 a.m.

This is when we have family Bible reading or discussion of anything pressing. We typically will read one chapter together, discuss, pray, and go on our way.

After Bible time, my husband works, my Bigs begin a load of laundry, clean up breakfast dishes, feed the animals, and go do school (usually in their room or basement), and my Littles are ready to start their day.

During this time, we prepare food for the day. Lunch items like rice or beans are perfect for cooking early. Dinner items like meats or soups are easily made at this time as well. The Littles finish unloading the dishwasher, gather remaining laundry, and water our plants. This is not playtime, and the children know that when they are done with their chores, we begin our school day. My Littles all have their own duties to do, and they do them each day.

10:00–10:30 a.m.

This is when we begin our school day with the Littles. We start by sitting down in the living room and doing our Bible lesson. Bible is always first because it's the most important. If you get nothing else done in your day, Bible class is the one you should aim for. Because we are doing Bible class on video, it gives me time to shower or finish any dinner plans, garden picking, cleaning, or a quick phone call. It's also a great time to get some sit-ups and push-ups in.

11:00 a.m.

Once the Bible lesson is over, we move on to our remaining subjects. I like to do reading lessons with my two smallest children, while the third does schoolwork independently. When reading is finished, we work on other bookwork until lunchtime.

12:00 p.m.

Lunch time. Everyone meets for lunch. We discuss our school and anything else that we can laugh about. After lunch, the Bigs do some clean-up while the littles play outside, or have Lego® time on rainy days. Rainy days are also a great time to play educational computer games for computer learning. I prefer this to be free-play time for my littles.

1:00–3:00 p.m.

Rest time for the two littlest, school time for middle, and school time for Bigs. This is also the time that I use for my business. In fact, I try to work from 1–5 twice per week if I can plan ahead. My children know that they cannot interrupt me. If the school gets finished, the remainder of the rest time is for reading only. If the Bigs finish school during this time, they do their chores, music practice, or exercise.

I also like to use this time to take a thirty-minute walk a couple of times a week. It's easy to do some more in-depth learning for your business while you walk on the treadmill. You may also have client phone calls while you are walking. Utilize time, sister.

3:00 p.m.

Snack time. Everyone always wakes up and comes running for snack time. I'll typically have my Bigs make a snack for my Littles, but if you don't have Bigs of your own, it would be easy to have string cheese and an apple on hand. After snack time, we have a history or literature lesson. I like to listen to our history lesson on audio to get some sit time in for the children. This also allows me to finish whatever business project I was working on before snack.

4:00 p.m.

Errand time. If we are going to go to the library or the grocery store, this is the time of day that I prefer to do it. If I'm not doing errands, the children have free play time while I do other things that need to get done. I do things like meal planning, garden tending, cleaning, etc. This is also a great time of day to connect with the older children, give them jobs to do with the business, or have a phone call with a friend. The children can also play computer games or do a typing lesson at this time. We greatly enjoy using YouTube channels for art learning and extra science lessons.

If I have a babysitter or grandparent that is planning to spend time with my children while I work, this is the time that I plan it. I will also often use this opportunity for busy boxes for my Littles. I'll talk more about this later.

6:00 p.m.

Dinner time. We all convene for dinner at this time. After dinner, we clean up and usually do something together, whether it is a game or a movie. Sometimes we go for walks, and sometimes we even exercise together. If the Bigs have youth group, this is when they would leave to do that. My husband and I love to communicate during this time, and we have two hours of just being together as a family without distraction.

8:00 p.m.

Bed time. This is when the Littles go to bed. I'll try to get some work done after they go to sleep. I'm usually in bed sleeping by 9:30–10:00 p.m. Sometimes you'll find me up until 11 p.m. though when I'm finishing a project.

9:00 p.m.

Curfew for Bigs. Just thought I'd mention it.

This schedule is fantastic for a Monday–Friday routine. It allows about fifteen to twenty-five hours' worth of work per week. Some parents even choose to continue through Saturday with Sundays off. You'll learn to greatly appreciate the freedom it gives you from complaining children, because they will automatically go to the next structured part of your day. It takes practice, but it's well worth the effort.

Any grandma time or weekend time is a bonus for work. If you have a co-op or playgroup your children get to attend, use that time for action! If you have plans in the morning for your children to have a playdate, use this time. You'll get tasks done while they play, and you can swap your school to the afternoon.

Fifteen to twenty-five hours might not be enough work time for you during the week. Sometimes I also have that dilemma. During these times, it's perfectly acceptable to work for an entire day once per week. Older children can do school without your help. However, younger children need something to do. During these days, I will ask a grandparent or a friend to spend time with the small children for one day per week (I usually do Fridays). If you are comfortable with a daycare setting, this is also an option, but my least favorite.

You can do this, mama. It is totally possible to run a business and homeschool your children.

If you have very young children who are not school age, here is a small list of ideas that I have used successfully during the school day. These are great ideas to gain time for work, or to help my other children during homeschool lessons.

Practice Sit Time

Practicing sit time is extremely beneficial for the brain of the child. It teaches them self-control and gives them the ability to be creative. Before I have the children sit, I give them a project. I lay a blanket on the floor for them to practice. They must stay on the blanket at all times during sit times. I'll set the timer for them for a short time. For the duration of the timer, they can do the project I have given them quietly as long as they do not leave the blanket. For very young children, this needs to be practiced to work up to the desired time. I talk in detail about projects and how I structure my children's sit time in Chapter 2: Structure.

Movie in the Afternoon

After naptime, let them watch a movie or educational show. I never allow my children to watch TV or be on a device before naptime (other than schoolwork). Otherwise, we find that children struggle to be kind during the day. In Chapter 2: Structure, there are more ideas on educational videos.

Naptime or Reading Time

This is an absolute must. If your child doesn't nap, they still need rest time. They need a good two-hour reset time. Let them have books on their bed, but make them rest. This would also be a great time to play an audiobook for them while they are in their bed resting.

Creative Time

This is a great time to get out the washable markers and a stack of coloring books.

Not Alone

The final thing that I'd like to share with you in this chapter is this: don't do it alone. If you are choosing to homeschool your children, find a parent in your area who homeschools successfully. As uncomfortable as it might be to "force yourself" into someone's life, decide to become friends with someone you can learn from. In Chapter 3: Relationships, I discuss friendships and healthy relationships that help you to learn.

If someone begins a diet, they are most successful if they do it with another person. This is why there are diet support groups. It's the same with an exercise program. People hire personal trainers not for continued exercise tutorials, but for being held accountable and consistent support.

The Apostle Paul, the greatest evangelist in the New Testament, brought friends with him on his missionary journeys. In fact, his dependence on his friendships significantly helped him to be more successful to reach more people.

In Acts 18, we learn that Paul left his friend Silas behind in Athens and went ahead to Corinth to preach. While he was in Corinth, he met a man who was a tent maker, and allowed Paul to work with him (Paul was a tent maker by trade). Paul was able to do ministry in all of his spare time, but he was limited because he still had to make a living with tent making. Silas and Timothy eventually met up with Paul in Corinth, and the Bible says that Paul was able to "spend all his time preaching the Word." I assume this means that Silas and Timothy worked on tents for Paul so that he could put everything into the ministry. By Paul's friends coming to support him, Paul was able to take the gospel further than imagined. If we imagine the scene, I bet that Paul was greatly encouraged by the presence of his friends. Imagine the deep conversations, thankfulness, and prayer they would have had together. Paul needed this support of friendships to continue his work successfully.

Still considering paul, there are multiple times in the New Testament in which he asks for prayer. He is constantly thankful for the support and friendship received from the churches. He never leads someone to think that he can do things on his own. Rather, he is an excellent example of how important it is to depend on others in important matters.

People are always most successful when they are supported by friends. Don't try to homeschool without support. You've got this, mama!

Points to Ponder:

Where can you improve or begin right away in your homeschool?

What are the things you've learned that you'd like to implement soon?

What is the most important part of the day in your family?

How can you use the most important part of the day to structure your household?

Write a daily schedule that includes school time and work time.

Chapter Ten

Gaining Traction

The last chapter of this book is dedicated to gaining traction in your life. Whether that's in homeschooling, running your business, caring for your relationships, or parenting, you need to move forward. If you get balanced in every area of your life, you will be able to enjoy it. However, if you want to gain traction or move forward, there are some things that I'd love to share with you.

> 1 Peter 4:10, "As each has received a gift, use it to serve one another as good stewards of God's varied grace" (ESV).

We all have natural gifts given to us by God when we become Christians. Just like our fingerprints are different, our gifts are also diverse. With each person's special gifts are likes, dislikes, tendencies, habits, fears, and joys. All of these things make you into a unique person that God wants to use to accomplish amazing things.

When we are using our gifts and doing something according to our personalities, we are unstoppable. But sometimes we get caught up in the weeds of "all the things that need to get done." This is a hindrance that we all face, whether homeschooling, parenting, or building a business. However, we can meet these hindrances with a plan—and I want to show you that plan today.

1 Corinthians 13 is the quintessential passage of Scripture about love. In this chapter, we find a list of what love is. This chapter is talking about love, but it's deeper than that. What this chapter is really saying is that anything outside of love is void. It's worthless. God wants us to be so focused on love that we naturally become loving.

When we are doing something that is focused on loving, we stop being so consumed with "me, me, me, me." To gain traction in your business, while being balanced in every area of your life, you must look outside of your own four walls and let yourself be a little bit vulnerable while loving others.

Consider other homeschoolers first. When you support other homeschoolers, you are helping them stay at home with their children. You are helping them survive this crazy world and train their kids in moral values. You can support homeschoolers by hiring them to do projects for you, and also if you are the one who is hired. Remember, what Paul said:

> 1 Corinthians 12:7, "A spiritual gift is given to each of us so we can help each other" (NLT).

The Bible repeatedly emphasizes the importance of fellowship and supporting each other. In everything we do, it should be evident that we do it for Christ.

> Colossians 3:17, "In word or deed, whatever you do, do everything in the name of the Lord Jesus, giving thanks to God the Father through him" (ESV).

Let me give you an example of helping others in love that I discussed today with my friend, Michelle.

You've already met Michelle - My sweet friend who teaches me things about others that I sometimes can't see. Michelle gives horseback riding lessons, she is a gardener, homeschooler, and makes homemade dinners. She loves to camp and is a sucker for any outdoor activity. A tomboy at heart, Michelle has been gifted four children, of whom three are rough and strapping boys.

My sweet, tomboy friend is also a beauty consultant. It seems like a joke, but it's true. In fact, because of her tomboy personality, and the surprise of recommending beauty products, she gets a ton of attention. She has gained immense traction in sales simply because of her nature.

In her business, along with sales, she should be coaching other women. However, Michelle has found that coaching does not come easily to her. In fact, she feels that her lack of coaching is holding her business back. Instead of being frustrated, or giving up, Michelle has a new plan. She has hired someone to coach her clients for her. Yep—she can keep on selling, and she can still grow her business. In fact, her home business is exploding because she has filled both the sales and coaching roles. By investing in another woman (in love, trust, and kindness) who can use her gifts, Michelle can get twice the work done.

It doesn't stop at business growth for Michelle. In fact, she is beyond blessed because now she can work with another woman who strengthens her character. She can love more and focus on her weaknesses less. She doesn't need to spend extra hours on her business but can continue to devote her time to her family.

As her children grow, Michelle is learning of new opportunities that her children can participate in. Homeschooling is crucial to Michelle, and she wants to give her family as many opportunities for success as she can. By having a second set of hands, Michelle is freeing up her responsibilities to invest more in her children.

Giving Up to Gain Time

As I left the conversation with Michelle, I thought about all of the things that I have given up to gain time. For instance, I used to make my own soap. It's genuinely better for my skin than any other product that I've tried. However, I gave up soap-making to redirect my time. Now, I purchase homemade soap from another homeschooling mom. This allows me to support another homeschooler and gain time for my family. My investment in the homeschool soap producer is worth the return of my time.

Another example that I thought of was grocery shopping. In Chapter 5: Physical Health, I mentioned that I like to use a grocery pickup service. But did you know that there are also people who bring your groceries to your door? Grocery delivery usually costs a little more, and you should tip the delivery person. However, when I have used the grocery delivery service, I was amazed at the time savings I had. By tipping my delivery person $30, I saved three hours, thirty miles on my vehicle, and I didn't have to get the kids out the door. Thirty dollars gave me three hours. That's a fantastic investment! If I had the choice to work or go grocery shopping, I think that work would be the better choice each time.

Do you enjoy gardening? Planting in my vegetable garden has been one of my favorite things to do in the summer. However, I took it a bit too far for a few years. Instead of being happy with eating my home-grown food during the summer, I felt obligated to can and freeze it. Instead of planting a modest-size garden, I planted a massive garden to fill my pantry with food. Not only was the planting using my time, but the weeding and picking also did. During the canning season, every other objective was tossed out, and canning became my all-consuming chore. Even making spaghetti for dinner became a task because I had to make homemade sauce each time.

One day, I browsed the frozen food aisle at the grocery store and discovered that green beans were only $1.00 for a bag. They were already washed, bagged, and frozen. My mind immediately considered my gardening. If I factored in the cost of seeds, my time spent in the garden, the canning stove's electricity, and everything else that goes into freezing beans, I was definitely spending more than $1.00 a bag. This day in the grocery store, I realized my error. My time investment into my garden is good when I'm doing what I love. However, when it becomes an obligation and the rate of return (time spent versus money spent) is reduced, this is an area that I need to re-evaluate. Since this evaluation, I have simplified my garden. If I get a lot of produce, I use it or give it away. I might put a couple bags in the freezer, but only if I desire to. From now on, I am free from the obligation of storing food. This gives me countless hours of freedom, and I recommend it to anyone who is bound to the idea that you must store food from your garden.

When we lived in a rural area, it was an expensive place to get car repairs. Even things like oil changes were at a high cost and difficult to get an appointment. Out of necessity, we needed to change the oil in our cars ourselves. However, when we moved closer to a larger city, we realized that it was affordable to have our oil changed by someone else. We took advantage of this! If we enjoyed changing the oil, then we would make time for it sometimes. However, changing it ourselves only saved us about $10.00. Ten dollars to stay clean and avoid an hour of grimy work— yes please! Getting our oil changed is a good investment because it has a high return.

Insurance can always be a tricky project to tackle. However, there are ways that you can have insurance and excellent service that save you time and money. When our family found a local insurance agent (her name is Ana), it helped us in incredible ways. We call Ana for anything related to house insurance, car insurance, and life insurance. Our agent gave me her direct cell number, and I can call or text her with any questions. If I buy a car, she gets me what I need on the spot. If we have been in an accident, she tells us where to go and what to do. Because we handed all of our insurance needs to Ana, we never have to think about it. In fact, she even shops around for the best rates for us. If you've never used an insurance agent, look around in your local area until you can connect with one. You'll never wait on hold again when you need someone. The investment is worth the return of peace.

If at all possible, find ways to support other homeschoolers and small business owners in your effort to gain time.

If at all possible, find ways to support other homeschoolers and small business owners in your effort to gain time. Similarly to my friend who makes soap, I prefer to find ways to save time while hiring or purchasing my products from homeschoolers.

Investing in Business

In our culture, the internet is the place to do business. Since our recent pandemic, everything is moving to online sales. However, If you do not have a web presence, it can be a huge stumbling block of forwarding momentum. In fact, most potential customers will even find local businesses by Googling. If your business doesn't show up in the search results, you missed an opportunity. Big businesses have picked up on this trend and has created websites that "build a site in one day." However, it is never that easy. Once a site is up, you need to learn the program, add pictures, and add content. Want to show up on Google? You basically need a Ph.D. to learn code and search engine optimization strategy for that. How about Facebook ads, Google ads, or making your site secure?

If you spend all of your time learning how to build a website that will give you a good return, you don't get to spend time working on the part of your business that you love.

You basically need a "Web Agent" who can take your dreams and build it into a website that works. You can just call that person to make changes, and you don't have to worry about learning another step.

- Need a website built exactly how you want? Call your web agent.

- Need e-mail? Call your web agent.

- Do you want to add an appointment scheduling to your site? Call your web agent.

- Need help with Facebook ads? Call your web agent.

- Maybe you think your site is running slow… Call your web agent.

- Domain names, hosting, e-mails…what do I need? Call your web agent.

This is where I am giving you my shameless business plug: I am the web agent. Send me an e-mail, and I can rock your web world: *elizabeth@singlerdesign.com*

When we realized that other homeschoolers and parents were desperately trying to build businesses and run their homes with sanity, we knew that we could help them. Since the latest pandemic, we have drastically changed our direction to serve homeschoolers and business owners so that they can be successful. We believe that by helping you, we are loving you as 1 Corinthians

13 commands. We can give you our best, and know that you can homeschool and love your family during the time you save. It blesses us to help you this way.

There are many other ways that you should consider getting help with your business to bring you to the next level. One way is to get help from a virtual assistant. Many homeschoolers would love to help you by being an assistant. These ladies do everything from Facebook admins to typing minutes from podcasts. If there is a tedious job that must be done, please consider hiring a homeschooling mom who can do it. Please feel free to utilize our Homeschool Community and directory at:

www.Facebook.com/groups/HomeschoolDirectory.

Feel free to use it for your business growth as well.

Another way to stay focused and move forward is to consider a book-keeper or accountant. When we discovered that our accountant could connect and reconcile all of our accounts and businesses, we were incredibly thankful to have that off of our hands. Each month, I would spend hours pouring over ledgers, and at year-end, it was also a hassle. Since hiring our accountant, I don't even think about it unless I'm writing a check to her. Each month that I send her payment, I am grateful that I can focus on my clients, not on money. I genuinely recommend that you consider this as soon as you can afford to hire out your accounting. If your projects only require a book-keeper, I have met many homeschool women who do this for a living. They are affordable, and you can support another homeschool family.

Homeschool Investments

There are also multiple ways that you can invest in your homeschool for high returns. It's hard to imagine adding more to your homeschool when you are trying to build a business. However, I have some excellent ideas that you can do both! In fact, there are many women and Christian families who can help you in this area.

In most areas, there are local co-op classes available. I touched on this in Chapter 9: Homeschool 101. Typically these co-ops require that a parent be involved. However, if you are looking for a time to work, many local homeschool parents will take on a "parent role" in the co-op so that your children can be involved. Although kindness will keep a local parent from not charging, I would recommend compensating a mother for this. It will be such a blessing to her.

In many states, college courses are offered to bright high school students. This is an excellent opportunity for your children to get some college courses out of the way before they graduate high school. Many times, the local high school will even pay to send your children to the college. Find out if this is available to you. It's also possible to hire someone local (preferably a stay-at-home parent) to run your child to the college if close by.

There are a plethora of academy programs available for homeschoolers. This is basically enrolling your child into school, but they do it at home. Many of these academies are Christian based, so you have biblical teaching and moral instruction in their curriculum. These can be very pricy, but helpful if you can afford them.

Since the pandemic, many parents are homeschooling and don't know where to begin. Many homeschooling moms have created courses for parents and act as educational consultants. These are great resources to get you familiar with what is available to you and which direction to go with your homeschooling.

Grading tasks can be difficult for a homeschool parent to find time for. There are probably other homeschool parents in your area who would love to earn a little cash to grade book work for you. It's also an excellent job for an older child or grandparent to help in this area. I prefer curriculum choices that grade automatically. This allows me to have full control and access to my children's grading.

Teenagers are delightful people to invest in. Homeschooled teenagers are some of the most considerate and willing people that I know. They are always ready to go the extra mile and be helpful. They tend to love working with children and are very capable of teaching. If your children struggle in a particular subject or do not have time to do a course like art, or gym, consider hiring a teenager once per week. Tutoring in English or teaching an art class are great ways to help a local teen develop new character traits. It will also encourage you to see your child thriving with extra instruction.

In fact, if you have older children yourself, consider allowing them to tutor other children. This is an excellent way to teach your kids leadership skills and planning ahead for projects.

If you have young children, see if there is a local MOPS or playgroup that your Littles could be involved in. If you don't have time to take them, see if you can hire another homeschool mom to bring yours along. This will give your children socialization time with a trusted friend, and you will gain working hours.

I mentioned this in Chapter 9: Homeschool 101, but I wanted to repeat the blessing of audio and video learning. Libby is an app that you can download to your phone, and it is a free source of library books that you can read on a device. They also have audiobooks to check out. I use Libby every day with my children, and I love it. Also, consider other audiobook programs if you have different availability in your area. For free video learning, I like to use YouTube channels that other homeschooling parents have suggested to me. It's often only a conversation at a homeschool meeting that will give you a plethora of ideas for this.

If you do not have a streaming device, I recommend visiting your local library and getting educational videos.

Points to Ponder:

What areas in my life are taking too much time?

What can I cut from my to-do list?

What are the ways that I can move forward in my business?

What are the ways that I can bless other homeschoolers?

Are there any ways that I can invest in my homeschool while keeping my business schedule?

Connections

Homeschool & Business Support

Throughout this book, I have mentioned various books or websites that can be useful to you on your journey. They have been very helpful to me. I hope that these resources will be helpful to you as well.

Recommended Facebook Community for Homeschoolers and Business Owners:

www.Facebook.com/groups/HomeschoolDirectory

Recommended Web Services:

- SinglerDesign.com

Recommended Reading:

- *Women of the Word*: by Jen Wilkin
- *Trim Healthy Mama* plan: Pearl Barrett and Serene Allison
- *Atomic Habits:* By James Clear
- *The 7 Habits of Highly Effective People*: Stephen R Covey
- *Boundaries:* Dr Henry Cloud and Dr John Townsend

- *Winning with People*: John C Maxwell
- *How Successful People Think:* John C Maxwell

Recommended Adult Exercise YouTube Channels:

- Caroline Girvan
- Holly Dolke
- Pamela Reid
- Vanessa Bauer
- Mod fit
- Chloe Ting
- Pernilla
- Hannah Oberg

Recommended Children Exercise YouTube Channels:

- SlotJaw
- Moe Jones
- Popsugar Fitness
- Emi Wong
- Little Sports
- Zumba with Dovydas

Recommended Educational YouTube Channels:

- CrashCourse

- Homeschool Pop
- SciShow
- Mr. Demaio
- National Geographic Kids/NatGeo Wild
- Science Sparks
- Whiz Kids Science
- Geography Now
- Liberty Kids
- Doodle Academy
- Red Ted Art
- Art for Kids Hub
- Angela Anderson (Painting)
- Generaleuphoria
- Geek Gurl Diaries
- Thought Café
- Finding Stuff Out
- Jam Campus
- Smarter Everday
- Brain for Breakfast
- Smithsonian Channel
- Gross Science
- SpaceRip
- Deep Sky Videos
- Outback Wild Rescue

- Ten Minute History
- A Kid Explains History
- America from Scratch
- So that Happened
- Travel Kids
- Hooptakidz Lab
- Kid President

CPSIA information can be obtained
at www.ICGtesting.com
Printed in the USA
FSHW020958110920
73642FS